Paran

Ross Andrews

Paranormal
Tourists Guide To
London
Book 1

Paranormal - Tourist Guide To - London

Contents
Introduction

A Very Brief History of London

Chapter 1 Ghost Walk One - *The South Bank*
    Ghosts to be found on the South of the Thames
    Lambeth Palace, Imperial War Museum, Florence Nightingale
    Museum - St. thomas hospital, St.Thomas Street – Old Operating
    Theatre Museum and Herb Garrett, H.M.S.Belfast, Towerbridge

Chapter 2 Ghost Walk Two - *The North Bank*
    Ghosts to be found on the North of the Thames
    All Hallows by the Tower,St.Magnus the Martyrs, Old London Bridge,
    Coutts Bank, Birdcage Walk, Buckingham Palace,Natural History
    Museum, Victoria and Albert Museum

Chapter 3 The Spooky Venues
    The London Dungeons, The Clink Museum, London Bridge Tombs,

Chapter 4 The Museums and Attractions
    Sutton House, Apsley House

Chapter 5 The Pubs
    Anchor Tavern, Black Swan Pub, Bow Bells, Flask, George Inn,
    George in the Strand, Grenadier Pub, John Snow Pub, The Market
    Porter, Morpeth Arms, Old Queen's Head, Rising Sun, Spaniard's
    Inn, Sutton Arms, Trafalgar Tavern, Town of Ramsgate Pub,
    Volunteer Pub, The Viaduct.

Chapter 6 The Theatres
    The Adelphi Theatre, The Fortune Theatre, Her Majesty's
    Theatre,The Lyceum Theatre, Theatre Royal Drury Lane

Chapter 7 The Underground
    Bakerloo Line, Bank Station, Bank and Monument, Becontree,
    Bethnal Green, Covent Garden, Faringdon Station, Hyde Park
    Corner Station, Kennington Loop, Liverpool Street Station

About the Author
Conclusion, Thanks and Further Reading

Paranormal - Tourist Guide To - London

Introduction

Welcome to the superbly spooky spectacle that is London, actually that is rather presumptuous of me. I am assuming you are stood in a book shop somewhere in London, or even in the gift shop of one of the venues that feature in this book. If you are, then I hope you had as a good a time as I did in the London Dungeon, Tower Bridge, Various London Theatre's, delete as appropriate or add your own.

...Now if you are anything like me you have probably read the rest of this book before bothering to get this far in the introduction. I admit I am an amazingly impatient person and I would have wanted to get onto the ghostie spookiness, rather than reading the opinions of self important author. Well stick with the Intro if you can as there are certain aspects about the paranormal, and London that I should explain before you think I'm just another nutter that sees dead people. I now return you to your regularly scheduled book...

You may of course have bought this book before venturing to this amazing city, maybe to find somewhere interesting to visit, and to know all of its grisly history before you get here. In this book I am going to tell you the stories that feature in some of London's spookiest, freakiest, and most haunted locations.

Some of these venues will charge you an entry fee to get in, but believe me most of the time it is well worth the fee just to experience the building let alone the ghosts. I have also included free places to go to, and a version of a couple of ghost walks which I suggest doing on a lovely summers evening, though in this country that can be a rarer thing than a ghost to find. Though if you really are interested in a proper ghost walk then I thoroughly recommend the walks done by Richard Jones, either in his book or actually guided by him in real life

Paranormal - Tourist Guide To - London

http://www.london-ghost-walk.co.uk/

This is not my first book on the fascinating world of the paranormal, and you may consider that a shameless plug - especially if you are heading out to Oxford, the Forest of Dean, Cheltenham, and many other places of haunted interest, as I have written books about all of those. This book however is going to concentrate primarily on places that you, as a paranormal tourist in our capital city, can actually visit for yourself.

The most paranormal thing about the London eye is that it is still standing, it was technically only supposed to be there for a year. Thankfully it is still an amazing piece of engineering and will stand for many years, making it 'London's Eiffel Tower'.

I have included when possible, the prices, and opening hours of venues. I am fully aware that you may be reading this hundreds of years in the future, as you are studying at school, the collective works of the genius that is is Ross Andrews. More likely you found an old book in a second hand book store, or down the back of the fridge.

So the year is 2011 and these were the prices at the time of writing I am sure that the more expensive venues will still be the more expensive venues in ten years time, and the price differences will also be in comparison to each other whenever you are reading this. So these facts are only here for reference and I suggest that you double

Paranormal - Tourist Guide To - London

check for price increases and opening hours/access restrictions

Now the amount of stories that I have been given before I even started doing any research is phenomenal in itself. I know there will be many paranormal researchers reading this book who stop and say how can you have a book about London and miss out …. Or not talk about … they didn't even mention … Well let me tell you that this is hopefully the first volume of many. I have written many books yet I have never seen so many stories to be found in one town or city.

So here we are with a collection of questions surrounding this book.

When possible I have gone and checked out the stories for myself.

Where are the ghosts? Well there is no point telling you stories about a nameless house in a nameless street so I will be as precise as possible. I will try and tell you what room, staircase, field, or graveyard, in whatever pub, museum, or churchyard you are stood in. Sometimes however there are stories with vague addresses this is done for the privacy and feelings of the families involved, not all people in this world are like us, some do not actually like the freaky weirdness that we enjoy.

How do I get there? I hear you ask. Whenever possible I will do my best to put the local buses or tube stations.

Why is it haunted? This is a much harder question to answer. If there is a story attached to a place saying that some ghost has returned to avenge its murder or to help tourists find the nearest toilets then I will put that. The problem is to answer the why question, means that I know what a ghost definitely is, and none of us (as I will explain throughout the book) can tell you what a ghost is.

Who is the ghost? A lot of the London stories have very specific ghosts attached to them, it may be Anne Bolynne the ill fated queen, or Jack the Ripper victims, maybe the ghosts of tourists who are stuck on the underground desperately trying to find the correct station due to line closures, or even due to the fact that I gave them wrong

Paranormal - Tourist Guide To - London

directions.

In my years of experience there are two types of ghost hunter there is the avid professional hunter who must buy all the latest pieces of high tech' gadgetry, needing a night vision camera, infra red motion beam barriers, and thermal imaging equipment. These people return again and again to the same venues to get more and more data trying to build up some form of scientific database. From the groups I have worked with I have found fifty percent of them are excellent and the other fifty percent don't actually know how any of it works, at least not correctly, or even where the batteries go.

The other type of ghost hunter is the most prolific the 'paranormal tourist'. These tend to carry nothing more than a pen and paper, and maybe a camera between them all. They genuinely hope to see a ghost, but just as important, is to try and tick off as many haunted venues as possible, on some form of haunted house shopping list. Perhaps they are producing their own version of the classic 'I SPY' book series, 'I Spy Paranormal Activity'.

Statue guarding London bridge, although it didn't do too good a job as it did 'fall down'

Both types of ghost hunter are catered for in this book. BUT! I also wish to open up my weird and wonderful world of ghost hunting to the general public. Every time you go visit a stately home, or castle, the one question you want answered is, 'Is It Haunted?'. I Hope to give you some form of insight to the facts about the murders, murderers, and ghouls that inhabit the fantastic historic city streets of London,

Paranormal - Tourist Guide To - London

making the average 'tourist stay' just that little bit more interesting. This way you may get better acquainted with the ghost that haunts the theatre where you saw that fantastic west end musical. You will find out about the phantom that frequents the museum you spent the day in, or even that the shadowy figure you saw on the streets has been seen by hundreds of other paranormal tourists.

Remember when you read these stories they are true tales told as accurately as I can. Nothing in this book has been fabricated by myself , I have never made up a story or expanded on the truth, or even exaggerated on a tale in anyway. I am fully aware especially as I go through all these tourist sites that people may be lying and telling me false stories to publicise their venue I will do my best to investigate and get to the truth when I can.

There are very sceptical people out there who will claim that ghosts do not exist and that I must be mad. I do actually admit I may be mad, but to say that a ghost does not exist is in itself madness, if you ask any of your friends you will find that about one in five of them will tell you a ghost story happened to them, and pretty much all of them will tell you a paranormal tale that happened to someone that they believe was not lying.

One of the scariest things you may ever see whilst ghost hunting − Me, in a Viking helmet (Don't ask it's a long story!)

It is not possible to say a ghost does not exist, in the same way that you cannot say U.F.O.'s do not exist. A U.F.O means an unidentified

Paranormal - Tourist Guide To - London

flying object, it does not mean little green men from Mars flying spaceships, so by definition of the actual words, unless you can identify it flying in the sky, it is a U.F.O.

Apply this same logic to ghosts, most people use the term ghost to mean a paranormal happening. When ghosts are reported to me they may be full apparitions that look like real people, it may be a strange mist or lights, there may be a poltergeist throwing things around, there may be something that makes the temperature drop to freezing in a heated room, there may be voices, noises, and strange sounds that cannot be explained. Anything paranormal is put down to ghosts haunting.

So you tell me what a ghost is and I will tell you if I believe in them or not. It is a long leap from believing in the paranormal, to assuming that it is the spirit of a dead person coming back to haunt somewhere from some form of afterlife.

So join me and make your own mind up in what may be the most haunted city in the world. Happy Spook Spotting!

The circular building near the bottom is actually Shakespeare Globe theatre

Paranormal - Tourist Guide To - London

Chapter 1
Ghost Walk 1

The South Bank

Well this is the first part of our investigations into the Paranormal so let us start on the South Bank. When we walk through the ghost walks what I am going to do is say where you should go, and include tales of the paranormal that happen to coincide with where we are. The problem we have is that many of these venues have a separate section in other chapters, so you can either jump forward to the chapter in question or read the whole book first and then head off on the walks later on.

This is not a short walk and we encourage you to look on a map and see exactly how far we are going to take you, this way you can join the walk where ever you want, and do it in bite sized chunks, rather than all at once.

Because of the nature of the journey you will take around these venues it would be impossible to write an actual walk for you to take as that would probably take up the entire book. Instead we are going to write the nearest tube station for you, and put them in order from West to East along the south of the river. I do not suggest you can walk all of this in one day, if you go into the attractions then I suggest you do this walk over a few days, or travel via the underground, or bus between venues.

We are aware that even though the title of this Ghost Walk is the 'South Bank' several of these venues are 5 or 10 minutes walk from

Paranormal - Tourist Guide To - London

the river, but I can guarantee they are within walkable distance as I have visited them all and I have very dodgy knees having had four operations so far. So I do insist you do your research first by looking at a map and judging how far you want to walk. Having said all this it's time to strap on your walking shoes and head off, sandwiches, and map in hand.

LAMBETH PALACE
Anne Boleyn

Location: SE1 (Greater London) - Lambeth Palace, & River Thames near the building
Opening times: Lambeth Palace is not open to the general public though tours can be arranged by writing to the bookings department.
Nearest Underground Station: Lambeth North

Lambeth palace is a fantastic sight that is easily accessible to paranormal tourists, the only problem being that it is not too easy to get access to the inside of the palace. Yet this is not a problem as you will see later because part of the paranormal phenomena related to this building is actually on the Thames near the palace.

LAMBETH PALACE

The palace has been the home of the Archbishop of Canterbury since 1200 AD, and before anyone as pedantic as me starts laughing, I mean the position of Arch Bishop of Canterbury not the present Archbishop who would be by anyone's standards rather old by this

10

Paranormal - Tourist Guide To - London

reckoning. Now speaking of old it is though the old word 'loamhithe' is the origin of the name Lambeth, and actually means 'Muddy Bank'

You can often get access to the gardens easier than the palace itself. They contain a herb garden and also a rose terrace, they are also amongst some of the oldest and largest Gardens in London. Tours of Lambeth Palace itself are available, but the booking list usually fills up for the year very early on, so make sure you apply well enough in advance before just turning up.

There are however exhibitions that feature regularly in the Great Hall/Lambeth Palace Library throughout the year so you can at least get to see part of the building. You will hopefully also get to see some of the treasure's within the Palace, including Mary Queen of Scot's Execution Warrant, The Lambeth Bible - a book used and owned by Henry VIII, Elizabeth I and King Charles I amongst others.

The British historian David Starkey says of Lambeth palace, that it is,

'the only place in London where, right from the road, you are confronted by Tudor London'.

I think I take some form of perverse pleasure including many an intellectual in my books, as I am sure they would hate the fact that they are being used in a book about something so unscientific and full of black magic mumbo jumbo. I look forward to the time that I can quote Stephen Hawking about the likelihood of poltergeists, until that time arrives however let me tell you about one of the many sightings of a famous ghost.

Anne Boleyn is supposedly not only seen but also heard in and around Lambeth Palace, it is said that she is seen carried on a Thames barge from here to the Tower of London, where her journey and her life terminated. Apparently it has been reported that the palace also is haunted by the sound of Anne Boleyn pleading for her life to be spared.

Paranormal - Tourist Guide To - London

IMPERIAL WAR MUSEUM

IMPERIAL WAR MUSEUM
The Madness of Spooks

Location: SE11 (Greater London) - Imperial War Museum, Lambeth
Opening times: Open daily 10.00am – 6.00pm Last admission 5.45pm (closed 15, 24, 25 and 26 December)
Price: FREE!
Nearest Underground Station: Lambeth North
Website: www.iwm.org.uk

I do like a ghost story to start with the phrase, 'Years ago when this place and an insane asylum' and luckily for us this one can start in such a way. This was the site of the second Bethlehem Hospital for the Insane, and was also used by the women's Auxiliary Air Force during the fighting in World War 2. As far as I can ascertain it was the staff that were there during the War that started the reports of hearing screaming and ranting late at night. They also reported the perfect ghostly behaviour, that of clanking and rattling chains.
Security guards have also reported hearing the sounds of shouting and screaming.

These venues I find fantastic partly because the ghosts are interesting but also because the venue itself is interesting, and more importantly FREE! One thing you need to know about a lot of free

12

venues in London is that in the museums quite often there will be areas you have to pay for to get access, they often have a travelling exhibition or one off form of display and therefore have to pay to be able to afford these. Hopefully when this happens it will not be in a place that is haunted, but we have to realise to be able to keep access to these buildings free they do need to do these paid for options.

FLORENCE NIGHTINGALE MUSEUM - ST. THOMAS HOSPITAL
The Ghostly Nurse

Location:
Opening times: Daily 10.00 – 17.00
(closed Good Friday, Christmas Day and Boxing Day)
Price: Adult £5.80 Child £4.80 Concession £4.80
Family £16.00 (two adults and up to five children)
The cost includes a free audio tour for adults and children
Group booking admission prices -
Groups of over 15 are required to book their visit to the museum.
They only accept group bookings after 2pm as they have school groups in the museum between 10am – 2pm.
If you are visiting with a pre-booked group of 15 or more, they offer discounted admission
Adults £4.80 Concessions £4.00 Children £2.90
Nearest Underground Station: Waterloo (on the Northern line). Lambeth North
The nearest railway station in London Waterloo.
Bus routes: 12, 53, 76, 77, 148, 159, 211, 341, 363, 381, 543, 507, C10, RV1
Website: www.florence-nightingale.co.uk
Email: info@florence-nightingale.co.uk
The Museum is fully accessible for wheelchair users and has a wheelchair accessible toilet. There is a loop system for the hard of hearing.

The interesting thing about famous ghosts is that they tend to haunt more than one venue, and we have had many tales of Florence

Paranormal - Tourist Guide To - London

Nightingale being seen in various places, so it is not surprising that she is seen in the Florence Nightingale Museum. She is also spotted in the corridors of the St.Thomas Hospital itself. There is also a ghost seen in the original site of St.Thomas's Hospital in Southwark which we will talk about later in this chapter.

One nurse who trained there happened to know the author of Haunted Hampshire by Rupert Mathews, and he included in one of his books several quotes from this person.

"She was dressed in an old-fashioned grey dress down to the ground. She came round the corner from the corridor into the ward and looked about. Then she walked out again. I was only a student nurse at the time and was all alone on night duty. There was not meant to be anyone else about apart from me and the Sister that came to check up from time to time. I wondered who this lady was and followed her out to the corridor, but she had vanished. I was told by older staff that this was the ghost of Florence Nightingale."

According to records if you were treated by Florence Nightingale you were actually less likely to survive than if treated by someone else

Now I do not wish to have people claim I am stealing from someone

Paranormal - Tourist Guide To - London

else's book but I include this quote for one major reason. The person who saw the ghost did not claim that they had seen Florence Nightingale they only said that they saw the apparition of a nurse in an outfit that would be similar to that worn by Florence Nightingale. It is only on the recollection of the tale that this ghost then turns into Florence Nightingale because other people have put two and two together and made five. It may well be that this figure is in deed the ghost of Florence Nightingale, or it may be that the hospital like any other hospitals is full of ghosts, but this is the most famous one and people like to claim to see celebrities even if they are dead ones.

The amount of times I have read stories about the ghost of King Charles the first or Anne Boleyn is phenomenal, even to the extent of Anne Boleyn being seen as a ghost in two different places at once. So let us hope that this actually is the spirit form of Florence, and your visit to the museum may throw some rather interesting experiences your way. If you do ever experience any sightings whilst visiting these venues make sure you tell the people in the museums as they often write down the stories and I get sent tales from all over Britain this way, and you may get to feature in the next book. (My contact details are in the back of this book.)

Some people who have seen the figure claim that she is cut off from the knees down, and often give perfect descriptions of her face as that is completely intact. As far a\s I can ascertain the descriptions given do not match anyone who ever worked at the hospital which may ruin the ghost of Florence Nightingale theory. We may be looking at several ghosts as we have already mentioned as reports do vary sometimes.

One local legend has reported that patients who spotted this phantom woman have died soon after. Now the problem with this tale is that this is a story you hear from hospitals all over the country, and lets face it a lot of the time if you went into hospital you were not necessarily coming back out again, so to see the nurse meant that you were in a place that you were likely to die in anyway. I am sure that should you see the nurse nowadays you do not have so much to worry about so happy spook spotting with this one.

Paranormal - Tourist Guide To - London

WESTMINSTER BRIDGE
See later entry – Chapter 'The Thames'

If you are walking this tour there is a delightful walk all along the South Bank from the London Eye right up to the TATE modern. The Tate Modern is also free so can I suggest going in their for an afternoon as well. On this walk you will pass great sites and sights, including The National Theatre, the Golden Hinde, and the Globe Theatre.

The replica ship of the Golden Hinde – Well worth a quick visit if you want a great photo opportunity, It is even possible to be a pirate and sleep on board for the night.

16

Paranormal - Tourist Guide To - London

*The Globe theatre from an old print,
Now either the people back then were about 10ft tall
or the scale and proportions are slightly wrong in this picture.*

I did actually ask the theatre if it was haunted and they said no, but I also asked people who worked there and they seem to think otherwise, having experienced seeing strange shadowy figures.

THE CLINK
See later entry – Chapter 3

ST.THOMAS STREET
Old Operating Theatre Museum and Herb Garrett
The Footsteps

Location: 9a St. Thomas's St. London SE1 9RY
Opening times: The museum is open every day from: 10.30am to 5.00pm
We are open Bank Holidays except Christmas Day and Boxing Day
Price: Adult £5.90 - Child under 16 £3.40 – Concession £4.90 – Family £13.80 (up to 2 adults and 4 children from the same family)

Paranormal - Tourist Guide To - London

Each group (of 10 or over) booking in advance will receive a free lecture/introduction to the Museum when the admission fee per person is paid as above.
Nearest Underground Station: London Bridge
Buses: Bus station and taxis in concourse at London Bridge Station.: 17, 21, 35, 40, 43, 47, 48, 133, 141, 149, 343, 381, 521, RV1
Website: www.thegarret.org.uk

OLD OPERATING THEATRE MUSEUM AND HERB GARRETT

This fascinating old building has a few tales to tell. I would be very surprised if this place was not haunted, or at least that people think that it is. This unusual place has an operating theatre at the top of the tower and is well worth the entrance fee. The Old Operating Theatre Museum is certainly one of the more intriguing museums in London. It has the oldest operating theatre in Europe and is possibly in one of the most unusual places as it is to be found in the Herb Garret of St Thomas Church, and was part of old St Thomas Hospital.

Richard Jones tells us in his excellent book, 'Walking Haunted London' that there is a strange haunting atmosphere that seems to permeate the operating theatre sometimes, and that strange noises are heard. Mike Barrell has worked there for many years and tells how he has frequently heard footsteps climbing up the staircase when the museum is closed. One time he and a colleague were alone in the building after a late night function in the museum, when they heard someone run up the stairs heading towards a storeroom. They naturally assumed that someone from the party was still in the building and headed off to find them. The door however was locked and there was no one to be seen.

Its not unsurprising that reports of ghost nurses have also been given, and some say it could be the ghost of Florence nightingale though this would seem highly unlikely as they do not think she actually worked here.

LONDON BRIDGE TOMBS
See later entry - Chapter 3

LONDON DUNGEON
See later entry – Chapter 3

HMS BELFAST

Paranormal - Tourist Guide To - London

HMS BELFAST
Strange Noises and Shadows

Location: Morgan's Lane, Tooley Street, London SE1 2JH
Opening times: Open daily 1 March - 31 October: 10.00 am - 6.00 pm (last admission 5.00 pm) 1 November - 28 February: 10.00 am - 5.00 pm (last admission 4.00 pm) Closed 24, 25 and 26 December
Price: Admission Prices 2011
Adults £13.50* - Child (under 16) FREE - Senior/Student (60+ years and students with identification) £10.80* - Disabled £8.10* - Unemployed £6.75* - Groups (reduced rates for groups of 10 or more) - Adults £10.40 - Senior/Student £9.10
Children but must be accompanied at all times when exploring the ship

*Voluntary donation
Your ticket price includes a voluntary donation (To help upkeep of the ship). And, if you are a UK tax payer, your donation will enable us to claim Gift Aid on your entire admission payment.
Admission prices excluding voluntary donation: Adults £12.25, Senior/Student £9.80, Disabled £7.35, Unemployed £6.10
Nearest Underground Station: London Bridge

Tales of spooks are hard to come by from here, as it seems many people are rather tight lipped about their experiences, but one person broke ranks and I was given some fantastic tales about the ship.

Apparently there were certain parts of the ship that people were very reluctant to venture into, and certainly didn't want to go alone. They are apparently inexplicable strange noises that emanate from various areas of the ship. Various people had seen things and strange shadows move around the ship.

When I have visited the ship I have not as yet seen anything, but many of the people I know of that have previous connections with the ship all say that they heard weird noises and saw strange figures, so if you visit and have more luck than I do then please email and tell me of your escapades, as this is the first in a series of books, and we hope to

Paranormal - Tourist Guide To - London

update many of the stories with the new experiences of our hardened Ghost hunters.

TOWER BRIDGE
A Multitude of Hauntings

Location: Tower Bridge Road, London, SE1 2UP,
Opening times:
Summer Opening Hours
 April – September 10:00 - 18:30 (last admission 17:30)
Winter Opening Hours
 October – March   09:30 - 18:00 (last admission 17:00)
Price: Adults £7.00 - Children (aged 5-15) £3.00 - Students (with identification) £5.00 - Seniors (aged 60 +) £5.00 - 1 Adult & 2 Children £11.00 - 2 Adults & 1 Child £14.00 - 2 Adults & 2 Children £16.00 - 2 Adults & 4 Children £18.00 - Under 5 Free Disabled/Carer Free
Nearest Underground Station: Tower Hill
Website: www.towerbridge.org.uk

The easiest ghost to spot in London has to be the one on Tower Bridge and can be seen virtually every night.

Paranormal - Tourist Guide To - London

Now the world of the paranormal does not just have to take in such weirdness as ghosts, I have studied the paranormal for years and often come across tales about ABC's or alien big cats,. Now this means alien as in not supposed to be there, not green things flying in spaceships. The other major reports we get may be about green things that fly in ships, U.F.O's.

During 2011 there were many video's and photo's appearing all over the internet of spherical flying objects flying around the Tower Bridge area. Now the problem with this type of phenomena is that it is impossible to authenticate, and U.F.O.'s are spontaneous and never necessarily in the same place, so it is not as if we could set up camera's and witnesses to try and capture it on film.

I have seen many of the video's and photo's and interesting though they are I cannot say they are not photo-shopped pictures or video's done on home computers, but they are well worth looking at and there are many to found on youtube on the internet.

*Unfortunately in my shots I never managed
to catch a glimpse of the flying little green men from Mars.*

Paranormal - Tourist Guide To - London

Now I bow to the greater knowledge of Paul Tudor when it comes to flying craft. He is a fantastic ghostbuster that has an interest in military craft and knows how planes manoeuvre through the sky and can tell you a lot more about UFOs than I can so instead I shall concentrate on the ghost aspect of London.

Paul on the left and myself on the right trying to out-scare a ghost

The bridge is not the oldest bridge in London, but it is possibly the most famous Iconic structure across the river, and is often confused by the Brits as well as foreign tourists as 'London Bridge'. There is even a myth about the fact that a wealthy American gentlemen bought London Bridge thinking that he was actually buying Tower Bridge, and before you start emailing me, I do know that is just a myth and is not actually true. Now the bridge is not famous for it's ghosts but does consist of some great stories, and many people do not actually know that you can go into the bridge and walk across the upper parts, it is a fascinating building that is well worth a visit, so long as you are not scared of heights.

23

Paranormal - Tourist Guide To - London

The bridge was started in the late nineteenth century and was finished and opened in 1894. It is a beautiful sight, and I only wish that modern buildings would have such design and thought put into it. The walkway offers some fantastic views of London and the river, yet it is also an area where many staff have reported uneasy feelings, as though being watched, and not only watched but followed. Footsteps are heard by staff and guests alike when there is no one to be seen, the owner of the feet can however be heard as there is a spectre that likes to whistle as he walks along.

Some investigators have told me that they have been there and seen the lift move of its own accord, (yes I know this can happen with lifts) yet apparently this should not have happened as the doors opened of their own accord. One medium said that there were several ghosts here, now anyone who knows me will know that I rarely hold much sway in what mediums say as most of them tend to be doing it for a living and charge extortionate amounts to just tell you information that you could have sourced of the internet. I am sure that there are genuine mediums, or at least people who think that they are communicating with dead people and are very sincere. But here are what the mediums have said, - there are males entities that walk along on the upper sections of the bridge, and at least one of them is in uniform, though no description of the uniform was given to me.

Another figure seen in a particular outfit on these walkways is a tall dark figure in a top hat and cape, though this one has been seen a lot less often.

I have heard some interesting recordings of strange banging noises from the building during a visit by some ghost hunters, and though they could not explain it, and neither could anyone working there, we have to realise that the building is a huge machine with lots of working parts and bits of metal that can cool and heat up creating strange noises. Later on the recordings you can hear tapping, breathing, and scratching noises that are also apparently unexplained. Some mediums have claimed that it is the spirit of someone who killed themselves possibly by throwing themselves from the bridge.

Paranormal - Tourist Guide To - London

It may well have been a ghost that dates from the 19th of November 1894, during this time a dare-devil called Benjamin Fuller dived from the top of one of the walkways, this was all done as a publicity stunt. Apparently this man was known to the police as he had dived off of several bridges before. He had to disguise himself to be able to do this as he was so well known to the police. Unfortunately, the dive into the river was his last and it killed him - the coroner's jury recorded a verdict of "Death by Misadventure."

Another group saw figures and faces standing at the end of the walkways and when they approached they realised there was no one there and the face then disappeared. Another group got confused as they saw a male figure and assumed it was one of their group, and ignored it, until they realised that all their group were at the other end, and that they were the only people there.

The biggest problem with a lot of these venues is access, not many of the larger landmarks will let you come in after dark after hours, and a lot of people seem to think that there is some major money to be made by charging people for ghost hunting. I can tell you now, no one makes money at ghost hunting, and certainly not people who are genuine ghost hunters, but because of programs like 'most Haunted' and groups like 'Frightnights' more and more money is being asked by more and more groups thinking they can get rich quick. So often groups will find a time to go into a building when it is unlikely to be busy, and carry out an informal investigation without the buildings knowledge. I have been in museums and seen people suddenly reach into bags and pull out dictaphones, video cameras, and EMF meters, and start taking notes and photographs. So if you are planning a paranormal visit why not try contacting the venue first and find out when it is normally the quietest time.

Interestingly the walkways were closed at one point around 1910 partly because of the suicides but also because it seems the local prostitutes liked to use it to meet their clients, and this attracted even more crime in the form of pickpockets. I am assured that this behaviour is no longer happening on top of the bridge, so bad luck if that's the reason you were going there.

Paranormal - Tourist Guide To - London

DEAD MANS HOLE

Under Tower Bridge we find a very interesting sight – DEAD MANS HOLE. Tower bridge became a favourite hotspot for suicide jumpers, and they tended to get washed up on the side of the river, in and area known as Dead man's Hole. It was a mortuary built into the base of one of the towers, and as far as I know this makes the only bridge in the world to have its own mortuary. Apparently this is where the poor suicide victims were laid out awaiting collection by their relatives.

There is a sign here that tells us of this history:
"The site was formerly used to retrieve the many corpses that were thrown into the river from the tower and surrounding districts. They were stored in the mortuary below until they were removed for burial."

The reason they would wash up here because of the shape of the river the tide made the bodies gravitate towards the area of dead man's hole. This seems to be one of the most feared and terrifying area of the bridge complex, and strange noises have been heard in the mortuary itself.

I was sent the footage from the Mortuary when 'Most Haunted' visited, and they did a Ouija Board here, I am not a fan of Ouija Boards and find them to be pointless, and certainly Ouija boards on television as a

Paranormal - Tourist Guide To - London

form of entertainment are completely useless from an evidential point of view. If you want to see their investigation just go onto the internet and you can watch the entire episode. Personally I do not find the Ouija board a great investigation tool. During their séance they heard things fall or get thrown and made contact with various spirits, some of which take over and possess Derek Acorrah the show's resident medium at the time.

As I said I do not hold much by the Ouija board but it is well worth watching to see Derek do his 'fake' possessions, and before you fans of Derek start writing to me, (or even his lawyers) I am only quoting the people who worked on the show, including Yevette Fielding herself.

TOWER BRIDGE

Paranormal - Tourist Guide To - **London**

Chapter 2
Ghost Walk 2

The North Bank

Yet again we have a collection of ghost sites that are now on the North Bank, but be aware if you wanted to do these as one Ghost walk you are not going to get much time in each venue as this is a very long walk. Starting at the tower of London, and ending up miles away on the other side of the city at the museums quarter, at the Natural History and Victoria and Albert. So please look at a map beforehand and see how much of this you can walk, and whether you should be taking tubes and buses.

ALL HALLOWS BY THE TOWER
The Were-Cat Lady

Location: Byward Street, EC3R 5BJ
Opening times: See website for worship and visiting times
Price: FREE!
Nearest Underground Station: Tower Hill (District and Circle Lines)
Website: www.ahbtt.org.uk

This church has an amazing history, partly because it is so old. There has been a church here dating from 675 which makes it the oldest church in the city. The great and the good have walked through this ancient churches door, including American presidents in 1797 John Quincy Adams the sixth president. Also we have an old spooky acquaintance that we have come across haunting many other venues

Paranormal - Tourist Guide To - London

that of the infamous Judge Jefferies. Samuel Pepys is supposed to have viewed the the great fire of London's devastation in 1666. He is supposed to have said of what he saw that it was, "the saddest sight of devastation."

One of the most famous stories of haunting in this venue goes back to 1920, and concerns the choirmaster and a rather spooky fan of church music. It transpires that the choirmaster and choristers went into the church one early evening and had been singing for twenty minutes or so, when they noticed an elderly lady standing about 8ft from them listening to the music. One of the choir boys fetched a chair for her and she sat down and continued to listen to the music.

The choirmaster later stated that the lady was dressed in what he described as old fashioned clothing. Now I have no idea what old fashioned clothing is to a man over a hundred years ago, and unless we have the worlds oldest choir master we can't exactly ask him today. He did say that her hair was grey and her face had shallow features. He did claim to be mystified by the old lady, partly because the choirmaster was certain that he had locked the doors, also the room they were rehearsing in had very creaky squeaky doors and he also had not heard any footsteps approaching from the old woman.

The practice eventually finished and the woman vanished, no sooner had she gone when a strange scratching noise started up in the corner of the rehearsal room. Then a cat was spotted running out of the room and go down towards the south aisle. On searching the church hoping to let the cat out they realised that all the doors were still locked and no old lady or cat was to be seen.

The cat may possibly have been the ghost of a cat attributed to a previous organist from the church, and perhaps it was this organist who was also the lady ghost. Five years after the first sighting, an old man spoke to the choirmaster and said that sixty years earlier he had been a choirboy at the church and the choir back then was led by a rather odd lady organist by the name of Miss Liscette Rist, who had a fondness for cats. He seems to have described the old lady and that this corresponded with the clothing worn by the apparition. She was

Paranormal - Tourist Guide To - London

apparently a huge animal lover and she even took on the personal task of sanding the road from the docks up to Tower Hill so that they did not slip whilst working.

It seems that the old lady left instructions for the cat to be interred in hallowed grounds in the church after she died, the vicar at the time did not follow these wishes and it is thought that this is the reason for the feline fright. Now I am pretty sure that the old lady organist was not a were-cat and unfortunately this old lady has not been seen very often since 1920, but the cat has been seen slightly more frequently however I do not think the cat is going to answer our questions.

This is a prime example of the fact that many people may have seen a ghost and not realised. There may have been hundreds of sightings of this cat and yet people might not have been aware that it was actually a ghost. I know of many sightings of ghosts in a particular haunted venue that I often investigate, and it's not until you start telling people about the ghosts that they say that they have seen them as well. Most people think that what they saw was real until you tell them that they were the only people in the building. So lets hope more and more people visit this place and see cats, now if you do then please check with whoever is working there that there is not a cat on the premises just to be sure.

ALL HALLOWS BY THE TOWER

30

Paranormal - Tourist Guide To - London

ST.MAGNUS THE MARTYRS
The Ghost of Miles Coverdale

Location: Lower Thames Street, London EC3R 6DN
Opening times:
SUNDAY at 11.00 am: PARISH MASS & SERMON
Tuesday at 12.30 pm Low Mass
Thursday at 12.30 pm Low Mass
Friday at 12.30 pm Low Mass
(usually followed by Benediction)

Wednesday at 12.30 pm, Holy Communion is celebrated at St Mary Abchurch.

*Please note that from August 4th - 28th the Tuesday and Thursday midweek Masses will be suspended.
The church is open for visiting and for prayer Tuesday to Friday 10.00 am to 4.00 pm

Price: FREE
Website: www.stmagnusmartyr.org.uk

This church I am sure looked great at one point, and I have seen old paintings and illustrations of it, all of which show a great structure which was overpowering all the surrounding features. Unfortunately nowadays it is virtually impossible to get a decent view of the building. It is amazing to think that this building now dwarfed by the surrounding structures was once the tallest structure by far along this road.

St.MAGNUS THE MARTYR

Paranormal - Tourist Guide To - London

One fascinating thing about this church is that in the churchyard you can see a few of the remaining pieces of Old London bridge, which by the looks of it has well and truly fallen down. This was one of the churches rebuilt by Christopher Wren after the Great Fire of London in 1666. There is a great figure in the world of religion buried here, that of Miles Coverdale, the man who gave the world the first English Bible. His tomb (dated from his death in 1535) has had reports from visitors to emanate a sense of woe and sadness.

Mile Coverdale was previously a rector of the church before going on to become the Bishop of Exeter, so perhaps he likes to return every now and again to make sure everyone is sticking to his book.

It may be him perhaps that haunts the church, but it is an unidentified figure that haunts, and the description given is a ghostly figure with dark or black hair wearing a cowled cassock. That's when he has hair as he has actually appeared without a head at least once,It has been spotted near the tomb but also on other occasions around the church.

There have been many witnesses including church wardens, workers, rectors and even a previous rectors wife have all testified to seeing the spirit on his ghostly visits.

There are only a few pieces of London Bridge left and these are about it.

Paranormal - Tourist Guide To - London

OLD LONDON BRIDGE
Screaming

Location: St.Magnus the Martyr – the churchyard has some remaining pieces of the bridge, but the hauntings are in the general vicinity of the river.
Opening times: Always
Price: FREE!

Way back as far as the 13th century the people of the Jewish fraternity were being prosecuted, which is no surprise they seem to have been attacked everywhere they go.

In 1290 all of the Jews in England were expelled from the country, and were forced to leave most of their belongings behind. A lot of them took what they could and headed to Poland on board a ship. This ship however sank and it is thought that you can hear their screams and woeful crying echoing down through the years.

If you are looking for the Old London bridge look for this sign.

Paranormal - Tourist Guide To - London

COUTTS BANK

Location: 188 Fleet Street WC2
Opening times: N.A.
Price: N.A.
Nearest Underground Station: Temple
Website: www.coutts.com

Coutt's bank is not exactly the place you could walk into with a pound coin and say, "Give me an account, you want my business", for one of its most illustrious clients is Her Majesty Queen Elizabeth II.

I have been reliably informed that the bank does indeed believe in spooks, as they once called in a medium to help out and rid them of a phantom that was roaming their building. And causing problems in their computer room. The Times reported that staff had complained of supernatural annoyances with strange happenings, and lights turning on and off, as well as the appearance of an apparition. Now in London we seem to have a large collection of headless spooks, and we are not short of one here either.

According to the medium this was the spirit of Thomas Howard the 4th Duke of Norfolk and his earthly living form existed between 1538 and 1572. He was executed because he planned to marry Mary Queen of Scots, and depose Elizabeth. The medium claims to have managed to persuade the dead Duke to pass on to some form of spirit plain, now not only did he achieve this amazing task but he did it in the presence of the current Duke and and Duchess of Norfolk.

My favourite aspect of this tale however is that when reporters asked the present Duke about it all at the end of the séance, he replied that he did not actually believe in ghosts.

Paranormal - Tourist Guide To - London

Annoying not haunted, Big Ben is not actually visible in this photo. Most people think it is the name of the clock, when in reality it is the name of the Bell inside the clock tower.

BIRDCAGE WALK
The Headless Lady

Location: St.James's Park, SW1
Opening times: N.A.
Price: FREE!
Nearest Underground Station: St.James's

The unusually named street is so called because this was the location of the royal menagerie and aviaries, it was developed here during the reign of King James I. Later King Charles II expanded the

Paranormal - Tourist Guide To - London

aviary during extensive reworkings of the park in 1660

The general public were not allowed here right up until 1828 when it was opened up to the public though by the middle of the 19th Century the fame it held was more for a place for homosexual liasons.

There is an old tale of a haunting from the 1800's, where a member of the Coldstream guards ended up in hospital with 'fright' after seeing an apparition. There was even a military enquiry because the two were so adamant about what they saw. This is a ghost that is not too common any more but I would love to experience this one, as it seems to have jumped straight out of a Stephen King book, these are the kind of sightings that ghost hunters like me crave every day.

At about 1:30 am on January 3rd 1804 George Jones of the Coldstream guards saw a headless woman rise from out of the ground directly in front of him. At no point did he do the soldierly thing and say 'who goes there' or 'friend and foe' which lets face it would have been pointless as something without a head is highly unlikely to answer you. The main reason however that he did not question the spirit was because of the fact that he had been temporarily struck dumb. I do not unfortunately have the military report in front of me but in one of the multitudes of books I have on ghosts of London there is a quote giving a description that he observed for up to two minutes before it disappeared:

*Admittedly it's not this woman that appeared as a ghost
but she can probably see you from up on her pedestal, as you cross the park
and birdcage walk*

36

Paranormal - Tourist Guide To - London

'... the figure was dressed in a red stripped gown, with red spots between each stripe, and that part of the dress and figure appeared to me to be enveloped by cloud...'

Now this did happen two hundred years ago, and I am sure that a guardsman now would be far more critical, and probably with a greater grasp of science, and explanations of the unusual and strange. Yet Apart from hallucination, it defies a simple explanation, I cannot think that someone seeing something two foot in front of them would be easily tricked by some simple trick of the eye, or a shadow that is casually glimpsed.

This womanly figure has been seen several times over the years only it seems to flee from the park and is often seen wearing a light coloured dress. One driver claims that he thought he had run over the ghost. He described it in a light coloured dress that was spattered in blood, and more importantly the figure was headless.

Theories about ghosts are more abundant than the ghosts themselves, but this one seems to be dated from 1784, and is claimed to be the headless victim of another of the Coldstream guards, this time there was a sergeant who killed and decapitated his wife, and tried to dispose of the body by throwing it into the lake in the park.

BUCKINGHAM PALACE

Location: Buckingham Palace, SW1A 1AA
Opening times: 23 July to 3 October
Price: The State Rooms, Buckingham Palace (includes audio guide)
Adult - £17
Changing the Guard - Free
The Royal Mews - Adult - £7.75
The Queen's Gallery - Adult - £8.75
Nearest Underground Station: Victoria, Green Park and Hyde Park Corner
Website: www.royalcollection.org.uk

Paranormal - Tourist Guide To - London

If there are any gullible American millionaires looking for somewhere to stay in London I have the rights to sell Buckingham palace, but I have been instructed to only sell it using cash, in a dark alley late at night with no witnesses.

There are two main ghosts that haunt this palace, and it is possibly because the building itself is not actually that old. Many tourists come to this country because we have a royal family, and our monarchy goes way back hundreds of years. In reality this branch of the Royal family have not been around that long and Buckingham palace has only been the official royal residence since 1837. King George II however did buy Buckingham house for Queen Charlotte in the 1760's.

So do we have the ghost of long dead Kings and Queens, I'm afraid not instead we have two very famous stories. One tale is

Paranormal - Tourist Guide To - London

of a Major John Gwynne, who was private secretary to King Edward VII, he was involved in a divorce case and could not cope with the glare of public scrutiny and shame and decided to end it all, and it is reported that the gunshot from his suicide can be heard repeating again and again through time.

The other story is supposedly of a Monk that lived in a monastery on this land before the Palace was built. Unfortunately it does not actually look like this monastery actually existed. The Monk however has been seen many times, it reportedly haunts the balcony overlooking the garden and arrives on Christmas day.

I have not bothered writing to this establishment asking if I can come in on Christmas day with my night vision cameras and recording equipment as I think I may get a possible 'NO!'

NATURAL HISTORY MUSEUM
Flashes and Doors

Location: W8 (Greater London) Cromwell Road, London SW7 5BD
Opening Times: Monday to Sunday 10:00 - 17:50
The Museum is open every day except 24-26 December.
Last admission is at 17:30
Price: FREE!
Nearest underground station : By tube within walking distance of South Kensington station on the District, Circle and Piccadilly lines
By bus Routes 14, 49, 70, 74, 345, 360, 414 and C1 stop near by.
Some tour buses also pass nearby
Website: www.nhm.ac.uk

Many ghosts have particular behaviour attributed to them, in pubs it is often reported that the entity will turn taps on and off in the cellar, and a regular one I have heard of in galleries and museums is an entity turning lights on and off. In the Natural history museum we have tales of such behaviour.

Paranormal - Tourist Guide To - London

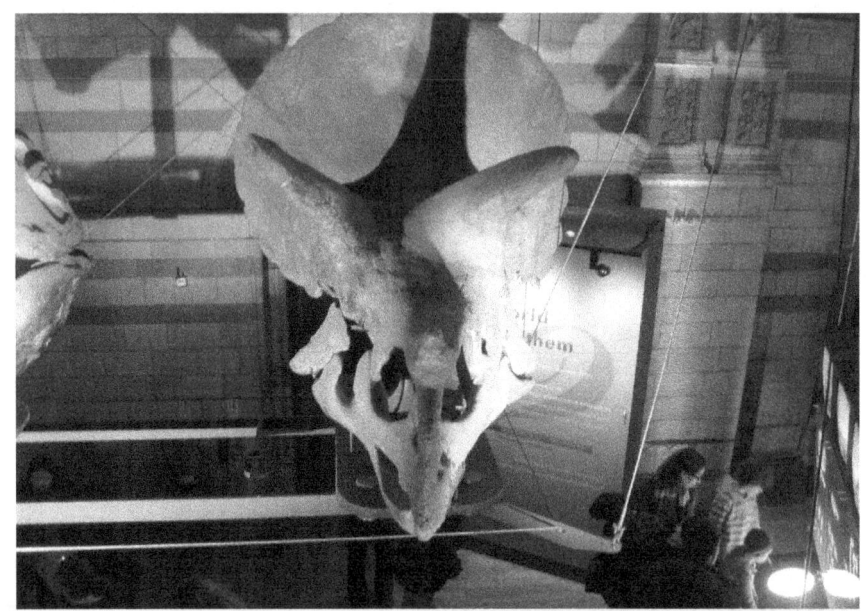

Not a huge amount of spooks, but there is a huge amount of Skeletons and Bones. The dinosaur exhibit alone is worth the visit.

Technically this building is full of death, when I went there I walked in to be confronted with the very large skeleton of a dinosaur. I cannot emphasise how much you should visit this area of London. Not only is there the Natural History museum but also the Science Museum, and the Victoria and Albert Museum all within 500 yards of each other. More importantly they are at the time of writing this book, free to get in to.

Well our light flashing ghost is reported in the Entomology Library, but he or she does not just confine themselves to this electrical activity. It is the other behaviour that drew me to this haunting, otherwise I would have put it down to faulty wiring or dodgy light bulbs. It is also reported that the doors are locked and unlocked by unseen hands.

This may be the same ghost that haunts the Waterhouse building only this time it has hands that can be seen, and they are the hands of a lady, as she is reported to be a female phantom.

The amazing site that greets you as you walk into the museum, there are so many Dinosaurs on display, but do not forget to look at the smaller displays there are excellent Monkey skeletons swinging from the ceiling

VICTORIA AND ALBERT MUSEUM

The Great Bed

Location: SW7 (Greater London) - Victoria & Albert Museum
Opening Times: 10.00 to 17.45 daily
10.00 to 22.00 Fridays (selected galleries remain open after 18.00)
Closing commences 10 minutes before time stated

Paranormal - Tourist Guide To - London

Closed 24, 25 and 26 December

The tunnel entrance to the V&A is open from 10.00 - 17.40 Saturday to Thursday and 10.00 - 20.00 on Fridays but may be closed on occasion on the advice of London Underground

Price: FREE!
Nearest Underground Station: Ten minute walk from Knightsbridge underground station (on the Piccadilly Line)
Website: www.vam.ac.uk

   The Victoria and Albert Museum is a truly amazing building and you could spend many days wandering around looking at the amazing artefacts. One of particular interest to paranormal tourists is that of a rather cursed bed.

   This bed was called the great bed, and when you see it you will understand why, it is enormous. Jonas Fosbrooke was the architect of the bed and apparently his ghost would attach anyone who decided to sleep in the bed, unless they were of royal blood. His snobbery however ended if his ego was flattered for if you drank a toast to him before lights out then he would leave you alone.

VICTORIA AND ALBERT MUSEUM

Paranormal - Tourist Guide To - **London**

Chapter 3
The Spooky Venues
The London Dungeons, The Clink Museum, London Bridge Tombs,

The London Dungeons

Location: 28-34 Tooley Street London SE1 2SZ
Opening times: Check website as they vary throughout the year, but you are generally alright if visiting between 10am and 5pm and avoid 24th Dec, 26th Dec, 31st Dec, 1st Jan as this year those dates the building is not open.
Price: Adult (16+) £23.52 Child £17.52 check the website for cheaper tickets and offers
Nearest Underground Station: London Bridge Underground Station (Northern and Jubilee Lines)
Website: www.the-dungeons.co.uk/london/en/index.htm

   Do not get too disturbed or confused at the thought of the London Dungeons, many a person may come along thinking that it is an old castle, or torture chamber, that is dripping in gory history. In reality the dungeons are actually the spaces underneath the arches of railway tracks going in and out of the station nearby. This does not mean however that it is not haunted, there have been buildings, life and death for many hundreds of years on this site. What there is now however is an amazing horror attraction, the first time I went here was many years ago, and it was a vastly different attraction. Back then the dungeon was more of a museum to horrific things that have gone of throughout the years, with models portraying various aspects of gore and torture, such as the black death and witch burnings. There was a small separate part that had an exhibition about demons, and my brother was too scared to walk in through the door.

To be fair to my brother he was actually only about 7 years old at the time and fair enough that a large talking demon that you could only get to through a tunnel of skulls would be rather disturbing to a small child. I did thoroughly love it, though I am may be seeing this through rose tinted spectacles and in reality I was probably just as terrified.

Since those distant dusky days of my childhood the Dungeons has changed and become more of of interactive experience, it has many live actors walking around, and instead of being allowed to wander around where ever you so desire, you are shepherded around in groups. This is fair enough as there are many actors and guides that talk to you and tell you of the amazing things that are in the attraction. Much that I loved the original dungeon if it was run that way now you would probably never get in, the queues can be very large, and inside it is amazing I could easily stay there all day.

LONDON DUNGEON

The inside exhibits change from time to time, but there is normally a collection of torture implements as you walk in to peruse your way through. Whilst inside there are things such as a Jack the Ripper

Paranormal - Tourist Guide To - London

exhibition, various people dying from the black death, and other London related horrors. They have many dungeons around the country and abroad now, and the idea is to buy into the local idea of terror, so in Scotland you have exhibitions about Burke and Hare the grave robbers, and in London we have Jack the Ripper. Do not despair we will get onto the whole jack the Ripper thing later in the book, we could hardly talk about gruesome paranormal activity and not include the worlds most famous serial killer.

So most of the strange scary things in the dungeons are either mannequins or even stranger they are very enthusiastic actors enjoying making you jump and scream. So why are we here, well throughout the years there are many reports of unusual paranormal happenings throughout the maze of tunnels and spaces encompassing the dungeons. It has been a while since I have been here, but always worth a visit every year, as you will see something new every time. I once ran a laser arena, a large maze in the dark with people running around shooting each other with laser guns, and it was one of the most haunted buildings I have been in, one member of staff even had to leave because she could no longer do the job because of the things that she had seen and experienced. When a member of staff refuses to enter the premises you cant really employ them any more, well I have been told this has happened at the dungeons as well, with staff leaving due to be too scared to come to work. Which is not surprising when you have been told the stories about the ghost of children playing, and dark shadows walking around. So before we go into the specific ghosts let us tell you about the history of the area.

Paranormal - Tourist Guide To - London

This area of London was renowned for being an area of extreme poverty throughout the years, the south side of the Thames and in particular this area has been populated for longer than most other areas of London. There is not a huge amount known about the specific history here, we have to remember that history is written by the rich and victorious in society. The poor tended to worry more about staying alive, eating, and not dying from various diseases, so taking time out from starving to write about your life is low on the list of priorities. We do know that the arches were part of the oldest passenger train services in London, we also know that it has been used as stables, possibly an orphanage, and my favourite of all - a wine cellar. One must assume that the orphanage and the wine cellar were not at the same time, small drunk orphans running around the tunnels may be responsible for one of the regular ghosts that we shall come onto later.

There has been a great deal of death in this area, as years ago during the war it was used as an air raid shelter, and the most important thing about an air raid shelter in my opinion is that it can withstand an air raid. This shelter apparently took a direct hit, and it is said about 67 people died here, and not all the remains have been found. It is believed that some of their bodies are still behind the bricks in various areas.

Firstly let us get on to disease, the Black Death featured prominently in the poorer districts of the city so many a dying pauper would be found in this part of town, and before we head into the area of the dungeons that concentrates on the black death take a look around you. There may be a man with two children there, keep looking they may not actually be tourists, for this has been seen by staff and visitors alike, these three then also disappear. It is events like these that may be happening every day and are being completely ignored. If you see a man and two kids in low light in a museum you would naturally assume they are there enjoying a day out, even if they were dressed strangely or behaving oddly your brain would still probably just ignore it and get back to looking at the strange article on the wall or listen to the guide taking you around the attraction. For all we know this ghost has been spotted hundreds of times and completely ignored.

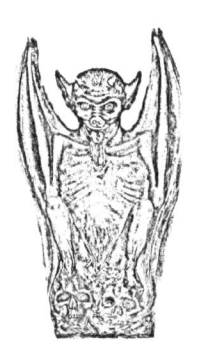

Another area that is a relatively recent addition to the dungeons, (hopefully you are still reading this book in decades to come so I will tell you it is 2010 when I am writing this) the boat ride – This may seem bizarre that there is a boat ride inside a building, but I thoroughly recommend going on it. Many people have reported the sensation of being watched, well firstly you are, there are going to be CCTV cameras around like on any other ride in a theme park, but ignoring me being facetious for just one moment people feel like there are eyes watching them as they venture through the tunnels. This may be just from the fact that you are confined into a space and in the dark, but the harder thing to explain is the weird whistling that has been heard in this area.

The area that I found the most intriguing is the mortuary area, many people have reported being touched and moved by unseen forces. I myself have experienced these type of phenomena in various places, and it can be very disturbing, if you are in the area when people have this happen you often see them turn suddenly, then look very confused because they are too scared of social embarrassment to say something just grabbed them. They would rather be molested by unseen hands than look slightly silly in front of strangers, the joys of the British reserve.

One medium, when he was on a well known TV show, told about how he saw a family in this room, and the man from the family was very angry. He seemed to have a massive chip on his shoulder about being

Paranormal - Tourist Guide To - London

poor in life, and that he hates rich people and people in their finery. This medium who apparently had not been told the tales about the models seemed to think that the man would move the models and push people around. The medium claimed that the name of the Male ghost was Cuthbert, and the scale of poverty going back not too far in history was immense throughout London so I think he does have the right to have a chip on his shoulder about it.

There are two mannequins dissecting a human on a table, and these have been reportedly moved by the ghost that is in here. Anywhere you get mannequins and waxworks you get these reports of moving figures, the scientific explanation is that in the dark slight eye movements, and the body swaying, creating the look of something moving when it is not. In Ireland there was a spate of miracle reports of a virgin Mary statue moving on a hillside in a grotto, I have seen some excellent footage of this happening. In reality the statue does not move yet on the soundtrack you can hear people all saying that they can see it moving slighting as though swaying in the breeze. We have a mixture of psychological expectancy and purely explainable physiology.

I put the above explanation in so that you think I do not believe everything that people say and that I do know my paranormal science, but after saying all this I will tell you this is not the kind of movements that have been reported about these mannequins. They move as though pushed by someone, and perhaps it is the 'someone' that has also been spotted occasionally stood in between these two models. Visitors have said it looks like there is another surgeon looking up and down the body, I am informed that even though a lot of performers end up working in the dungeons none of them are responsible or mistaken for the ghost sighting.

Many people have witnessed a tall dark man, this may sound like a good thing if you are a woman looking for your perfect man, but think again. He is not a pleasant sounding man, and has a woman already, he has been seen following a woman in Victorian dress they seem to be chasing each other. So are we witnessing our friendly mate Jack the Ripper visiting the attraction named after him. If you are in the

Paranormal - Tourist Guide To - London

Jack the Ripper area listen carefully as many people have said this is the area where children are heard and more importantly seen playing 'ring-a-ring-a-roses'. Many people will tell you that Ring-a-roses rhyme is actually about the black death and it symptoms, so it is not surprising if you see a collection of kids in a ring your brain associates the image with the rhyme. I would like to add that the rhyme was in existence way before the black death, but may well have been appropriated and changed to suit the disease and not the disease being the inspiration for the song.

Children are also heard crying in the dungeon's even though the building is closed and the general public are no longer on the premises. Perhaps they are experiencing the ghost of my brother crying as he was scared of the demons so many years ago. Alright I admit he didn't cry, and more importantly he is not actually dead, (unless you are reading this in the year 2089 and beyond, and they have not invented life extending technology).

There are also reports of screaming, and I have heard some great recordings of what sounds like people sighing and mumbling in various areas in the dungeons.

If you do experience anything in the dungeons make sure you tell the staff, and see if they can confirm your tales, there is no point telling everyone your amazing ghost story and then they go along one day and see a different actor or guide dressed as the same figure you described. Also this building has many strange noises due to trains nearby, cars driving passed, and general London noises, due to the shape of the rooms, tunnels and ceilings noises echo, amplify, and

Paranormal - Tourist Guide To - London

change throughout the museum.

I have been sent many files of strange audio recorded by people walking around the dungeons and similar buildings, if you plan on doing this make sure you try and tell me the details of the area the noise is in, if I get lots of files from the same place it makes it easier to investigate. If you send me photo's, video, and audio but do not give me much information then there is not much I can do with it.

Always try and collaborate your tales, and confirm their authenticity, and when you are sure there is no rational explanation for what you saw then and only then we draw the conclusion that something out of the ordinary has happened. Then MOST IMPORTANT of all email me and tell me about it

(**ghostnight@hotmail.co.uk**)

The Clink Museum

Location: *Clink Street between Southwark and London bridge*
Opening times: *Summer - July– September*
7 days a week 10:00 – 21:00
Winter - October – June
Mon - Fri 10:00 - 18.00
Weekend 10:00 - 19:30 (Closed Christmas Day)
Price:
Adults £7.00
Children (under 16) £5.50
Concession – Students, OAP, Disabled (I.D.required) £5.50
Family (2 adults and 2 children under 16)£17.00
website: www.clink.co.uk

An excellent attraction, and I am slightly perturbed to use the word enjoyable when you think about the suffering that went on in this Hell Hole. Originally it was part of the manor owned by the Bishop of Winchester and was used originally to house people like myself – heretics, but also people who disturbed the piece in the brothels.

Paranormal - Tourist Guide To - London

Many church men were involved in earning money from incarcerating people, and also running brothels. We have to dissociate our view of the modern church with what it was hundreds of years ago. Bishops and clergy were the centre of power in society and therefore there was a great deal of corruption and evil doing on behalf of God and the church. The prison was originally a single cell with a grille separating it from the real world, which eventually became separated cells, housing men and women. This place was renowned for the hideous brutality and torture that was handed out to these victims, and eventually became the slang word for spending any time in a prison or police cell, - to 'Spend time in Clink'.

So are any of the wretches that were incarcerated here still hanging around today. Well during my enquiries over the last few years I was told that several people, and that includes employees, have reported seeing a small girl playing with the chains on the floor, when she is spotted she is apparently wearing rags, and that also a priest-like figure has been seen, who can mysteriously disappear through the wall.

A boy is seen travelling through the museum and disappears through a wall, and another tale I have been told of the place is of a woman rattling her chains that are attached to her shackled feet.

Now what fascinates me is the similarity between the ghosts we have a girl in rags, and a woman who seem to exhibit similar behaviour, and a young boy and a priest figure walking through a wall. So are these ghosts the same figures just interpreted through different eyes. With a death rate of about 50% it is not as if we can route through historical records and try and identify the victims. So I am very intrigued to hear from any visitors as to what they see here, and see if we can shed la new light on the subject. Well it's good news at least for the male ghosts as they seem to escape from the prison through the walls, sorry ladies. I have been given reports of people who said they saw a figure near the 'torture chair', and strange misty figures seen in doorways.

So what have the ghost hunters found when they have visited, lots of investigators go to these venues in the daytime and try to sense spirits

Paranormal - Tourist Guide To - London

and investigate phenomena, they tend to avoid half term and if possible, school hours, so they can get the building to themselves.

Well one medium came in and started talking about a religious figure who walks around praying, and he is lost in this realm feeling deeply unhappy. He also picked up on the young boy who seems to run around and laughs, yet also feels as though this boy was under 6 and is sometimes scared. Other investigators claim to have heard chains rattle, and metallic noises which don't seem to have an earthly explanation. Quiet whispering voices have been reported in the building, along with grunts, and scraping noises.

There is a problem with all London venues when it comes to strange noises due to the fact that there are hundreds of trains running under the ground, cars driving, and water flowing, all of which can lead to very unusual noises vibrating through a building. So to make a really impressive piece of phenomena we need loud noises that must be definitely from within the building, and the groups, and mediums that have gone in hear often say the chain noise is rather loud. I have heard recordings from the building and there are tapping noises that seem to respond to questions as though answering, but we have to remember when the building has members of the public in it they could be playing with you, finding your investigation very funny. I have been on commercial ghost hunting nights and seen guests messing around by throwing stones and making noises, so always be sceptical when you can.

Now the problem with bringing a medium into a venue like this is that they can go online and find out about ghosts, or even read books like this. The worst I have seen are mediums who just walk around and read what's on the walls and displays and pretty much repeat it. My favourite (not at this venue) was a fake medium who was looking at a painting and 'psychically' came up with the name of the person in the portrait, even though it was written on the bottom of the canvas.

Having said all this I can honestly say that I have seen some interesting photo's and heard some intriguing audio from this venue that is not easy to explain.

Paranormal - Tourist Guide To - **London**

*Is this a genuine photo of a spook leaving the museum?
Looks unbelievably real to me, I'll let you decide*

London Bridge Tombs

Location: 2-4 Tooley Street, London Bridge , London , SE1 2PF UK
Opening times:

Paranormal - Tourist Guide To - London

Price: Child ticket - 5 to 14 years
Student ticket -15 to 17 years and students with valid student ID
Adult ticket - over 18 years
OAP ticket - OAPs aged 60 or over
Children aged 4 and under are given free entry to The London Bridge Experience however children under the age of 11 will not be admitted to The London Tombs.
Adult - £23.00
Child - £17.00
Student - £21.00
Family - £74.00
Nearest Underground Station: 50 metres from London Bridge Station: British Rail and London Underground (Northern and Jubilee Lines).
350 metres from Monument/Bank Station: Docklands Light Railway, London Underground (District Circle, Central and Northern Lines)
Buses:
21, 35, 40, 43, 47, 48, 78, 133, 149, 381
Website: www.thelondonbridgeexperience.com

OLD LONDON BRIDGE

Well this can be great and very disappointing at the same time, it is designed as an attraction for the general public as a 'walk through ghost train'. The problem with this concept is that these can be terrifying or just laughable depending on the people you are with, and your state of mind. The other problem with this venue is that it has

Paranormal - Tourist Guide To - London

companies running commercial ghost hunts, which can cost £75 or £85. Now if I pay this amount of money, I expect more than a bunch of strangers in a dark room pushing a glass around on a Ouija board.

So this is somewhere that can be experienced during daytime hours, but obviously you will not get time to do vigils and parapsychological experiments.

As you can see this is not a cheap day out, and many visitors from outside of London are often shocked by how expensive these venues are, so I suggest always looking on the internet for two for one offers and other special offer prices.

So now why would you come here? Is it haunted or not. Well its a highly entertaining and informative venue, and if you have visited all the others in the book then heading to the more expensive venues is worth a special look, for your birthday or a day out.

We are told that it is haunted and on the website to the venue it tells of a figure that has often been mistaken for a 'Lazy actor' who just stands and looks at you. The figure has been described as female, and often when she is reported the venue claims that there has been no female members of staff working in that vicinity. The staff have christened her Emily, and she seems to frequent an area that was used as a Plague pit. Obviously if you do capture anything on camera, or you experience anything you consider paranormal, please tell the staff as they will be able to inform you if anyone was in that area.

In my job as a paranormal writer I get sent links to footage, and clips from peoples video cameras all the time, and I have seen lots of footage from ghost hunts organised in venues such as these. Most of the time all I get to see are video's of the odd click, or bang noise in a dark room full of people who do not know each, and could be in various stages of drunkenness, or under the influence of drugs, or various religious beliefs. So most of the footage I get is worthless from a paranormal investigators point of view, having said all that I have seen many clips of people who genuinely feel they have experienced paranormal activity. There are recordings of wailing, whistling, and

Paranormal - Tourist Guide To - London

groaning, and people who claim to have seen figures, (seen only from the waist up) walk through walls.

Now with all the underground venues in London and other venues in the dark is that the other senses seemed heightened, so you will feel on edge and start to interpret noises as something other worldly when in reality it is something perfectly explainable. When underground the sound of cars, and trains travelling nearby will vibrate through the ground and move things. Now if you are in a tunnel the shape of the tunnel can make sound waves act in unusual ways, it can amplify, change the pitch, and intensity, and even make noises appear from somewhere completely different to where the noise is emanating from.

Clerkenwell House of Correction – Clerkenwell Close EC1

Unfortunately this building no longer has access, but there are some very famous tales associated with it so I thought it would be remiss of me not to include them.

Built several hundred years ago all that is left of the prison is the underground section, and was recently a museum, here there were over 10,00 men women and children held. This was used as a holding prison, and today's prisons are bad enough with people mistreating each other and abuse that goes on despite the best efforts of wardens, but in the 1800's the prisoners were brutally treated, and various attacks, and sexual assaults were rife in these environments.

This section was built in the 17th century and remand prisoners were kept here awaiting trial, so there is a distinct possibility that this place was full of innocent people who were easy pickings for many of the corrupt officials, and other evil tormenters that had access to them. Perhaps this is the reason that children can still be heard crying in the vaults of this evil place. Dark figures are seen wandering around, and upon investigation there is no one there.

The most disturbing looking figure that is seen through the tunnels is an old evil looking man, by the term old we probably actually mean middle aged. People would not have aged that well back then due to disease and hard living, but this man has an evil look to him, with shallow cheeks and a pale complexion and people think he may well have been a Prison guard. The reason I was told that ghost hunters have assumed that he is a prison guard is that he has been seen and heard throughout the tunnels therefore having free range and not being locked up in any form of cell.

It is assumptions like this however that create ghosts from nowhere. This is why there are so many ghosts of famous people, Anne Bolyenne seems to haunt many places, but not as many as Charles I. Everyone likes to think their ghost is important, and people start to associate stories that they can assume are correct, so a man in Civil War style clothing becomes Charles I because King Charles once stayed there, or a headless ghost is Anne Bolynne because she lived there and was beheaded. The same may be said for this prison warden ghost, we know the building was used as a prison so we put two and two together and create a character for this figure.

Before long the tale gets out on the internet and n books such as this and then the myth is created that the prison is haunted by an evil prison guard, this then seems to shape the sightings from then on. So the question is asked, do people create the ghost and in reality there is nothing there, or do people see something and imprint their own beliefs and thoughts on the image to create a spiritual persona. This line of inquiry could go on forever and I could write essay upon essay about the psychological aspects of haunting so instead lets get back to the gory scary stuff.

The haunted window, well I think that title says it all. The window seems to have faces that appear in it looking at you when there is no one there.

In the long ventilation tunnel on the far side of the building there is a gate that opens and closes itself, sometimes it has closed itself and then refused to open again, locking you into the prison as if you were one of the prisoners from times gone by.

Paranormal - Tourist Guide To - London

In the most haunted cell in the building people have seen an old woman frantically searching for something that she has lost, and visitors have reports trying to interact with her, but she ignores them and keeps on searching.

The 'Washroom' has another old lady in it, this time she stares back at visitors, shortly before disappearing, and if you fail to see her perhaps you may see the young girl that runs through this room before she disappears.

As with all underground venues the noises are prevalent, and the sound of shuffling feet has been heard when there is no one in the building, and I am told groups have heard moaning and groaning. I am yet to hear any of these recordings, but I have been told that very few paranormal investigations have managed to stay very long and have left rather scared, so perhaps there is not too much in the way of evidential recordings.

I have tried to regain access to this building but unfortunately the current owner does not want anything to do with paranormal investigations. I thought it a good idea to include it here however, as in years to come the building may change hands, and hopefully allow paranormal tourists once more. Please contact me if this is so and you get to visit, I always want to be kept undated on recent paranormal activity.

Paranormal - Tourist Guide To - **London**

Chapter 4
The Museums and Attractions

Sutton House, Apsley House

SUTTON HOUSE - HACKNEY

Location: 2 and 4 Homerton High Street, Hackney, London E96JQ
Opening times: Various see National Trust website
Price: adult £3, child £1, family £6.90
Nearest Underground Station: Bethnal Green (then 254, 106 or D6 to Hackney Central)
Website: /www.nationaltrust.org.uk

Unfortunately I myself have not managed to be able to investigate this building but I have been given a great deal of notes, history, pieces of evidence, and tales about this venue, and I cannot wait to get to this venue to try a little ghost hunting there myself.

I am a sucker for history I cannot get enough of old buildings and this one dates back to 1535, by one of Henry VIII's counselors Sir Ralph Saddler and was then altered in the 17th Century when it became two separate properties. Thankfully we can now get into the property as it is no longer a private residence, but are we alone here, or have the previous residents stuck around.

We have several spectres wandering around this building which is no surprise as it has been private houses, boarding school for young gentlemen, and an academy for girls. We have possibly two different

Paranormal - Tourist Guide To - London

ladies walking around this house, as there are reports of women in White and also Women in Blue, or maybe a ghost that likes to change its wardrobe every so often.

I was sent some footage from an investigator of someone calling out for someone or something to interact with them, and one of them says if there was anyone present could the spirit touch or move anything, within seconds the other investigator lets out a little scream as something grabs him by the shoulders. As I also do I like to try and explain the paranormal where ever I can, so to offer a rational explanation there is a thing that happens to the human body where muscles can twitch or spasm especially in stressful situations. If you have primed the subconscious with images of ghosts, and you believe that a ghost can grab you, then perhaps your brain is putting two and two together and making five. That does not mean that the man was not grabbed by a ghost, but as paranormal scientists we must always look at both sides, as it was once pointed out to me by someone who was rather annoyed at a dismissive sceptic.

My colleague said, 'There are not two sides to every paranormal argument there are three, and you should always try and follow the third, the first side of an argument is the believer who will believe that every little thing in the world that happens must be paranormal and caused by dead people coming to life again. The second side of an argument is the totally sceptical person that says if it does not fit within the the logical laws of science as he understands them that it cannot possibly be true. The third side is the best to take, neither believing the believers or believing the sceptical, it is possible that paranormal things happen but we do not have the understanding of the science as yet to fully explain them, and to dismiss everything is just as bad if not worse than to believe everything.'

So we have wandering ladies and possibly grabbing ghosts, but what I really like in this venue is the report of phantoms that are on four legs, that of several dogs walking round, barking and whining. I have spent many nights in a haunted building that has a large ghost dog, and it has been seen many times. Often this ghost is completely ignored as people think it is a real dog, it is normally the staff that

Paranormal - Tourist Guide To - London

report these types of haunting as they know there are no real dogs in the house at the time. Perhaps it is these dogs that other dogs see when they come into the building, the stories are that real dogs have come in and then suddenly stop as though staring at something and they wont go any further.

The ghosts supposedly belong to a clothing industry tycoon by the name of John, and he reportedly loved his dogs as though they were his own children. It is said that he preferred the company of his dogs than that of other people, and it looks like he has continued this after his death as well. Mediums have said that they believe that he is responsible for some of the poltergeist activity that has taken place in the building. There are windows and doors that open and shut on their own, and objects have been moved around, and thrown across rooms. Another well known phenomena that occurs around paranormal activity an poltergeist happenings is the sudden drop and rise of temperature, when there are no open windows, or obvious winds blowing around or through the building.

In one of the rooms, which is now an exhibition room, there used to be a bed and people who had stayed and lived there were woken up by the bed shaking apparently by a woman in Blue. She no longer can shake the bed as it is not there, but this has not stopped her visiting as she is seen walking around the room. In the photo's I have been sent from this room there is a painting on the wall with large staring eyes, this can make people feel uncomfortable and feel like there is someone in the room with them, creating a sense of fear and paranoia. I do not believe however that this could create the image of a blue lady, and the stories go back far enough and consistently enough to make me think small influences like these are not the cause.

I mention this partly to show the avid ghostbusters amongst us that you always must look for the logical or subliminal reasons behind a haunting before jumping to conclusions. The previous stories talk about the sightings of ghost dogs, and often the sound of dogs throughout the building, so we must look at the obvious and say well the coat of arms has three large dogs in it, is that the reason dogs are in my mind. Is the noise definitely in the building, often ghost stories tell us that the noise was faint, well if that is the case perhaps there is a dog barking half a mile down the road and the wind is in the right direction. To put your mind at rest however the ghost dogs I have been told about sound like they are actually in the room with you.

Let us head into a rather strange part of the building the Chapel, unusually this is under the building, most chapels take pride of place in any house and so they tend to be above ground with stained glass windows allowing colour and light into the building. The chapel in a basement is a rarity and normally was in a house where the religion had to be kept secret. I am not a religious man at all and I find it hard to understand how people were willing to die for their religions, and needed to find a secret place for worship, but we must remember our mindset has changed drastically in just the last fifty years, let alone the last few hundreds of years.

The haunting in the chapel however is not necessarily a haunting associated with death, this may be a prime example of a stone tape theory, which I shall explain in the glossary at the back of the book, but I shall summarise it by saying that a building can remember things and replay them, as if it has stored the event in its walls. In this room mediums claim there has been a fight and this replays so that people can hear arguing, and that this energy may be responsible for some of the poltergeist activity.

The activity that I have had reports and evidence from are so numerous I could not include them all, yet this building delivers on all paranormal levels, we have poltergeist, we have audio phenomena, we have light anomolies, we have physical interaction with people being grabbed and pushed. Remember these events have happened in the daytime every bit as much as when the building is not open to the public so this is a building well worth a visit by any investigator.

APSLEY HOUSE

Location: 149 Picadilly, Hyde Park Corner, London - W1J 7NT

Paranormal - Tourist Guide To - London

Opening times: 11am - 5pm
Summer Season: 1st April - 1st November.
Winter season: 2nd November - 31st March.
Closed on Mondays except Bank Holidays
Price: Adults: £6.30 Children: £3.80 Concessions: £5.70
Family Ticket: Apsley House is free admission to all on Waterloo Day
Nearest Underground Station: Hyde Park Corner
Website: www.apsleyhouseguide.co.uk

An unusual political ghost was seen here many years ago by the then unpopular prime minister The Duke of Wellington, at the time he was not the people best friend as he was opposing the reform bill of 1832, Angry mobs were starting to mass and it looked as though there would be a crowd ready to lynch him outside his house.

As he was ignoring the crowd and heading to bed he saw the figure of Oliver Cromwell standing in the corridor. The Ghost turned to him and pointed at the angry mob outside, and waved his finger disapprovingly at him. The Duke changed his mind straight away and the bill was passed.

Paranormal - Tourist Guide To - London

Chapter 5
The Haunted Pubs

With all these following stories I must admit I have not been able to verify every single one, and one of the venues got me rather drunk and I lost some of my notes. So to the best of my ability I have sourced and checked these stories.

Anchor Tavern, 34 Park Street, London, SE1 9EF

I am reliably informed that this was one of the favourite haunts of the writer Mr Samuel Johnson, he did mix in some rather dubious company however, as it seems that it was also a well known holt for smugglers and various vagabonds. In 1984 there were refurbishments done to the building and they manage to uncover various nooks and crannies which were supposedly used for such nefarious purposes.

Stories of ghosts are often from the animal kingdom, in fact in London we have a haunted zoo but more of that later. This pub has a haunting of the animal kind. A dog to be precise, but before I tell you of this dog I need to tell you about the history of the story.

Back in the 1700's there were things called press gangs, their influence and tales are greatly exaggerated. They supposedly came into a pub and kidnapped you to be in the Navy, often they were recruiting agents who would get you drunk and then when you woke up you were miles out to sea after having agreed to serve in the force. The tales of the press gang arriving, hitting you over the head and dragging you out of a building are often exaggerated though I am sure many underhanded things did go on.

Paranormal - Tourist Guide To - London

In this pub such tales of violent press gangs are abound due to the fact that one such gang had a battle on their hands when they entered this premises. A large dog belonging to a customer who was reportedly being press ganged decided that his master would not be dragged out to the ship and attacked the gang. One of the gang slightly alarmed at the protection his victim had managed to use the door to protect himself and slammed the tail of the unfortunate animal in the door frame and severed it completely off. The poor animal ran off yelping and whimpering and was never seen again. Never seen again in the living flesh that is.

The reports that I have been given are that around closing time this dog makes its presence felt again, it is seen and heard sniffing around looking for its tail or its master. So if there is a ghost of an RSPCA agent anywhere in London I will try and put them in touch with this pubs landlord.

Black Swan Pub, 148 Bow Road, London, E3 2SE

We have names, and dates with these spirits, who allegedly haunt the pub's cellars. They are Cissie and Sylvia Reynolds, both daughters of a previous owner of the pub. They were killed along with their mother when the pub was destroyed during a German Zeppelin attack back in 1916 on September 23rd. It dies not seem as though their mother has decided to come back to haunt the pub just the two girls instead.

Bow Bells, 116 Bow Road, London, E3 3AA

In my favourite haunted building, St.Briavel's Castle, there is a ghost that is generally only spotted by women as the ghost tends to shy away from men, particularly burly looking men. This pub has a similar ghost that is spotted generally only by women. Although the main reason for this is that it tends to haunt the ladies toilets.

It is a rather surprising form of haunting and not one that I have been

Paranormal - Tourist Guide To - London

able to investigate for myself due to the gender aspect of the phenomena. When you sit on the toilet it apparently flushes itself. That aspect of the haunting is slightly less alarming than the other reported type of haunting in the main pub, it is reported that a mist rises from the floor of the bar area.

Flask, 77 Highgate West Hill, London, N6 6BU

I have spoken in length about Hogarth and his amazing artworks in my previous book about Paranormal Oxford, well I mention him again as the 'Flask' is apparently a previous local of his. It is not him however that aunts this bar, and we know that for certain unless Hogarth was in to cross dressing. The ghost that haunts here is supposed to be that of a woman.

I have not been able to ascertain who the phantom is, but I have been told she may have been a previous worker at the bar, who ended up killing herself due to a failed love affair. This seems a perfectly plausible story except for the fact I was also told it may be connected with the bullet that is embedded in the 'snug bar'. This bullet seems to be the subject of many a conjecture and no one really knows how it happened.

Many ghost in pubs tend to move things around and this one is no exception. Not only do we get the stereotypical temperature drop so often associated with hauntings, but also the ceiling lights have been known to move of their own accord, glasses are moved by no visible means, and the freakiest phenomena of all the feeling of someone breathing on the back of your neck.

George Inn, 77 Borough High Street, SE1 1NH

This is I am told a very famous London pub, due to the fact that it is the last galleried coaching Inn in existence in London and was built in 1677. This building is reputedly haunted by a female misty figure.

Paranormal - Tourist Guide To - London

One explanation of who she may be is that of a former landlady a certain Miss Murray. One of the explanations for this is that she was running the establishment back at the end of the coaching era, and into the evolution of the train. She does not seem to be happy with progress as she has drawn a particular dislike to electrical items, and modern electronics. John Hal, one of the landlords over the years commented that, 'Anything electrical annoys the ghost, new tills will always go wrong. We call the engineers but they can never find any logical explanation or genuine fault. Computers are the worst. It can take months of engineers coming and going before they will work properly, and even then they will suddenly crash for no apparent reason.'

I thank Richard Jones for that last quote, from his fantastic book 'Walking Haunted London'

I have also been informed that the security cameras have picked up strange figures, and images before. Unfortunately like all these hauntings when I ask the ghost hunters if I can see the images no one knows where they have got to. This does not mean I do not believe them, it's just that a lot of people do not realise how valuable these things are. If you have genuinely thought you have caught something paranormal on tape please send it to me to analyse. So many people tell me they had some interesting footage but they taped over it, or can't remember where they put it, and the one I get all the time, 'yeah, no problem I will mail it to you' and then I never see it again. I am fully aware that the real world occupies most people's lives and they forget about these things, not realising how obsessed we freaky ghost hunters are in seeing this material.

George in the Strand, 213 Strand, London, WC2R 1AP

I am including this story because it illustrates the theory that ghosts do not necessarily have to have lived in a building to haunt it, as the ghosts dates from a building that was on this premises many years ago, this building having been built in the 1930's.

Paranormal - Tourist Guide To - London

Unfortunately my theory falls somewhat when I learned that the foundations of the building are from the original building when the ghost was supposed to have lived. These foundations are supposedly from an original building back in the 17th Century. These cellars appear to have an original resident still in it as a rather handsome smiling fellow has been spotted wearing the clothing that a Cavalier would look rather at home in. So unless we have a landlord or landlady that somehow likes to have the occasional Civil War themed party in the cellars then we have a ghost.

The building itself was built in the 1930's but the foundations upon which the pub stands belong to a much older building and date from the 17th century. And it is in the cellars that the ghost has quite often been seen. He is described as a handsome, smiling man who wears the clothes of a Cavalier.

Grenadier Pub, 18 Wilton Row, London, SW1X 7NR

I do like ghosts that stick to a nice timetable, as this one apparently does. Ghost hunting is a very boring hobby sometimes, most of the time you are stuck in a cold dark room waiting for something to happen. The chances of that something happening are often very low, with the ghosts being spotted once every couple of years. So it is always nice to have ghosts that stick to a pre-arranged schedule. These ghosts are often reportedly things like battles and skirmishes. There is a ghost of battle that is apparently supposed to happen on its anniversary in a small town called Tewkesbury, the problem is when we have gone to investigate it, there has been a medieval fair on the battleground site. The may well be a battle being re-enacted but it merges very well with the revellers all dressed in the same outfits who have all being drinking since ten o'clock in the morning and are now running around trying to mock kill each other.

So what does our helpful time keeping spirit do here. The back story is that this pub was the favourite haunt of gambling soldiers. One September a soldier was caught cheating at cards in this pub and his opponents beat his so badly that he died. He apparently makes

Paranormal - Tourist Guide To - London

himself known by moving objects, making things disappear, and tables rattle. When he is seen it is said that he is a solemn looking figure, and this figure may be responsible for the sound of footsteps emanating from the rooms, and possibly even the occasional unearthly moaning noises from the cellar.

One intriguing story I found was about a Chief Superintendent from Scotland Yard, he was drinking one night in the pub, I assume it must have been a night off and he was not on duty. You can see for legal reasons I know I have to cover myself here, I also think he was not a smoker, as he was surprised by smoke wisping around him. He reached forward to what he thought was the source of the smoke, and then retracted his hand in pain as he claims it felt like it was burnt by a cigarette.

So if you are here in September take your video cameras with you, and please email me the results. I only mean that if you get something paranormal, I don't really like sitting through hours of footage of your mate getting slowly drunk on his twenty first birthday. I also don't need to see cigarette burns unless they were definitely from unseen invisible cigarettes.

John Snow Pub, 39 Broadwick Street, W1F 9QJ

There was a great man in London back in 1854, a doctor by the name of John Snow. He was the genius that tracked down the source of cholera to a water pump that used to stand outside this pub. You will hopefully see a pink granite slab nearby that marks the spot.

It is highly unlikely that this great man is the man that haunts this pub. It is reported that there is a figure of an unknown person sitting in a corner who apparently glowers at the clientèle.

The Market Porter, 9 Stoney Street, Borough Market, London, SE1 9AA

This is not a ghost of a market porter it is however a haunted pub of that name. After hours neighbours have reported seeing figures floating around. Not just stragglers pouring out after a lock in these are strange looking floating people.

THE MARKET PORTER

The strangeness does not just stay outside however as in the pub the ghosts are not the most helpful creatures. One landlord spoke of how he had unplugged the dishwasher and in the morning not only had it been plugged back in, but the doors were wide open and the dishwasher and been turned on spilling soapy water flooding the bar. This ghost likes to play with electrical equipment as the landlord also told a tale of how one of his tills upstairs running all by itself. Well this would certainly cut down on the staff wages as I assume the ghost does not need paying, or perhaps he felt sorry for the mess he had caused with the dishwasher and was trying to work off the debt he felt he owed.

Morpeth Arms, 58 Millbank, Westminster, SW1P 4RW

Australian history owes a lot to the history of crime throughout London, many people were sent out there to cultivate the country many times under dreadful conditions and trumped up charges. What has all this got to do with our ghosts I hear you scream to me, well in this pub it apparently has a lot to do with it.

The cellar is supposed to have been used as a makeshift prison cell for someone who was waiting to head off on this perilous journey. It is told that he tried to escape, and not only was this escape unsuccessful, but it resulted in his death. The Staff think that this may be the story that is responsible for the hauntings in the cellar. I have been told staff are reluctant to head into the cellar and hooded figures have been seen in there.

This brings me onto the subject of hooded figures. There are huge amounts of records indicating that hooded figures are seen a lot more often that is statistically likely. If we think that a ghost tends to be from someone who had a violent death, or even if we just think that a ghost could be anyone from anywhere, then statistically you would expect a ghost to represent the population of the time. So unless hoodies were a huge fashion item throughout history there are a lot more hooded figures than there should be.

Paranormal - Tourist Guide To - London

MORPETH ARMS

When I examined this phenomena it seemed the hooded figure reports tend to say a dark figure or a misty figure, and it could be that the 'hood' may not be a hood but likely to be an indistinct shape and the human eye and brain turns this shape into a hooded head. The eye is designed to quickly see things, and then the brain turns this camera image into a recognisable image so that it can decide to run away or defend itself from a possible attack. This is the reason a fleeting glimpse of something vaguely human shaped in your mind can become a human or ghost, so if the top of the human shaped figure is not exactly head shaped then the brain thinks well it must have a hood or be wearing a hat, a soldier with a helmet, or something else that your brain would have a frame of reference for.

The ghost of a man, who died trying to escape from the cellars where he was being held waiting to be transported to Australia, haunts the pub. Staff are very reluctant to enter the cellars because of the atmosphere and cloaked figures that are seen.

Old Queens Head, 44 Essex Road, London, N1 8LN

Many places that I have investigated, and many places that I have been told tales about have ghosts of young girls, and nine times out of ten, they are described as girl between the ages of 8 and12 wearing a Victorian style night gown. This thankfully is one of the 'one out of ten' that is different. This young girl is apparently weeping and dressed in Tudor clothes, and she is seen in this pub.

THE OLD QUEEN'S HEAD

This is not the only female spirit seen in the pub as a woman is also seen. Perhaps it is these two spirits who are responsible for the doors that seem to open and close of their volition. They may also be running around the premises for they have been heard running in the passageways.

Rising Sun, 38 Cloth Fair, London, EC1A 7JQ

These rather unpleasant spectres seem to interact with the living rather easily, and scarily.

A former landlady tells a story of how she was having a shower one day, I hasten to add that is not the scary part of the story, that comes now. She was in the shower when something entered the bathroom.

Then in true horror psycho style the shower curtain was slowly pulled back and instead of a psychopath with a knife she felt an ice cold hand run down her back. Suffice it to say there was no actual living person there.

THE RISING SUN

There was also a time when several pub workers who all 'lived in' got woken up by the feeling that something was sitting at the end of their beds. This was made worse because sometimes the entity would actually move the bedclothes slowly off the bed whilst they were in it.

The sound of footsteps has also been heard by people in the bar as though the footsteps were going overhead, yet there is never anyone on the floor above, in the upstairs bar.

Spaniards Inn, Hampstead Heath, NW3 7JJ

Many ghosts have appeared because of women, or should I say many men have killed each other over women. This pub is actually named after such an event. Two former Spanish landlords fought a duel over a woman and it is said that one of the men is buried in the garden. One assumes that it was actually the one who got killed that is buried, and he is the one that haunts the pub.

This pub has its celebrity ghost as well, Dick Turpin is reportedly haunting the road outside the pub. I am not entirely sure if anyone knows what Dick Turpin actually looks like, so it may be a ghost pretending to be Dick Turpin. The paranormal equivalent of setting up a facebook page of someone famous and rather pathetically pretending to be them.

Well Dick Turpin may be a ghost here, and is dressing up as a woman in white and haunting the garden. As a female figure all in white has been seen, and an invisible someone appears to be grabbing people and pulling at their clothes perhaps he thought no one would suspect him if he was dressed as a woman.

Sutton Arms, 6 Carthusian Street, London, EC1M 6EB

THE SUTTON ARMS

I do like a haunting with a name, I have lived in a haunted building before and called my ghost 'George'. I have no idea why I called it George, there is no historical character that would have influenced this name, other than one of the King George's that had any reference to the building I was in. My brain decided that it was called George, and I hear time after time about hauntings and the house owners or staff in the building give it a name. This pub has such a ghost, this one is called, 'Charlie' he is like myself a smiling red haired man, but unlike me he has been spotted several times, and in several places around the pub.

One of the most cinematic stories I have heard was from the friend of the landlord, I say cinematic as I have watched many a horror film and this seems like a scene from one of them. The landlord's friend was combing her hair and looking in a mirror when she saw the red haired man standing directly behind her, she spun around to find herself completely alone. Then when looking in the mirror again he had disappeared from there as well. You can almost hear the soundtrack of psycho playing in surround sound.

Charley does seem to have a favourite table, somewhere in the corner of the pub, where he has been observed quietly sitting. The most frightening sighting that I have heard of here was from two women who were sat talking and he appeared sat between them, he turned to them smiled and then disappeared. I could not find out whether these two women managed to stay and finish their conversation or whether, like I probably would, run out screaming.

Trafalgar Tavern, 6 Park Road, London, SE10 9NW

This London haunted pub was built in 1837 and the site was also previously a hostelry that was called The George. The haunting seems to have originated in the original pub called the George.

This is yet another pub that used to attract famous writers as this one had not only William Makepeace Thackeray, but also Charles Dickens, and Wilkie Collins. Charles Dickens even featured the pub in one of his books 'Little Dorrit', now that must have been worth a free pint or two. I must admit I am hoping that goes for all the pubs that get mentioned in books especially by modern writers specialising in the popular paranormal science field.

When the spirits are present in this bar staff have said the atmosphere changes, and an icy chill permeates the bar. People have

Paranormal - Tourist Guide To - London

also reported seeing a figure walking briskly in the upstairs rooms. I'm sorry to report these rooms are not open to the public but do not worry because this bar has more than one ghost.

TRAFALGAR TAVERN

A man has often been seen, dressed in Georgian clothes and drinking a pint of beer. He sits either at the bar or at the piano. When he has finished his pint, he gets up and leaves through the fireplace which is where a door was once located.

A previous landlady also reported that she often experienced the figure and would always greet it nicely and say good morning to it. Assuming that this spirit had more right to be there than anyone else, it has been there so long it technically has squatters rights. Other members of staff have also reported beer crates lifting and moving of their own accord around in the cellars

Town of Ramsgate Pub, Wapping, E1W 2PN

This pub apparently claims to be the oldest on the Thames, and for our foreign visitors to the capital and are translating this book to their friends as they read it. 'On The Thames' does not mean there is a floating pub bobbing up and down on the river, though that would be an impressive ghost to see. If you email me with a phantom of a floating pub I think you may have been in a non floating version for most of the day examining spirits of your own.

Paranormal - Tourist Guide To - London

The pub was once known as 'The Red Cow'. The theory is that the name was in honour of a former barmaid who had a head of flaming red hair, and also must have been a bit of a cow by the sounds of it. The steps outside the pub are reputedly haunted by the infamous Hanging Judge Jeffries, and according to reports it is the Police who have seen this spirit as well as the pubs clientèle.

The problem I have with the ghost of hanging Judge Jefferies is that he does like to get around as I have investigated at least five different premises all haunted by Judge Jefferies and not one of them was the place he died in. Many ghosts are named after the most famous person who ever stayed anywhere near the building, as its more interesting to say Judge Jefferies haunts the building, than Old Bob the man who used to clean the drains.

Volunteer Pub, 247 Baker Street, NW1 6XE

This I have been told is one of the most famously haunted pubs in London, I rather sheepishly have to admit I had never heard of the place but did smile nicely and pretended as though I did so as not to disappoint the ghost hunter who was telling me. The pub stands on the site of what was a 17th century mansion, and this building was owned by the Neville family. This original mansion burnt to the ground.

Thankfully part of this building still exists, the lower part of the building as in the foundations. Many pubs have haunted cellars I have discovered, especially in the cities, they tend to be built on top of cellars, vaults and foundations of previous buildings. The Neville family Mansion cellars still exist, and so does at least one member of the Neville family. We are not sure which member of the Neville family but there is a description, they say that the ghost wears a surcoat, breeches, and fancy stockings.

The Viaduct, 126 Newgate Street, London, EC1A 7AA

Yet another haunted cellar here but with a much better history. This

78

was a former Victorian Gin palace, in Victorian times it appears that most of the London population were avid Gin drinkers. These cellars once belonged to the infamous Newgate prison, five of the original cells are now part of the lower floors of this pub. It is hardly surprising that these cellars seem to have some form of haunting going on, and what fantastic stories I was given about this drinking den. It seems the staff and locals have christened this ghost 'Fred' as yet I have not found out why.

One previous manager ended up joining the prisoners, and Fred, in a cell as the door slammed behind him, the lights also went off, and when he found the door, no matter how hard he tried he could not open the door. His wife heard him yelling and came to see what the problem was, she apparently managed to open the door without any problem.

Another tale is from a workman that was doing some form of work in the cellars when he felt someone tap him on the shoulder so he turned around fully expecting to see someone there, instead what he saw was a heavy rolled up carpet lift into the air with no visible means of propulsion, and then it fell to the floor. I was not told whether he ran screaming from the building or if he nonchalantly turned and finished the job in hand. My money is on the former scenario and not the latter.

Other strange things include a poltergeist that steals drinks, at least that might be the ingenious story that a rather drunk ghost hunter might tell people, and it also seems to turn off the lights in the ladies loo's.

Ye Olde Cock Tavern, Fleet Street, London, EC4Y 1AA

I have not heard many stories about this pub, but the one that seems to be the most famous is well worth reporting to you.

A girl who worked in the pub back in 1984 opened the back door to put out some bags of rubbish, and she screamed. We are told that she saw a grinning, disembodied head apparently floating in the mid air.

Paranormal - Tourist Guide To - London

She was obviously rather distressed and the landlady told her to go and lie down upstairs, the poor barmaid went up the stairs and screamed again, she was apparently standing in front of a portrait.

Because of this portrait she was later able to identify to whom the head belonged. It was the portrait of the writer Oliver Goldsmith who is buried outside the pub, exactly below where she encountered the apparition.

I myself have seen a floating head ghost and I can honestly say it is one of the scarier apparitions that I have encountered, I don't think I could ever identify the face though as I didn't stick around long enough to get a good glimpse.

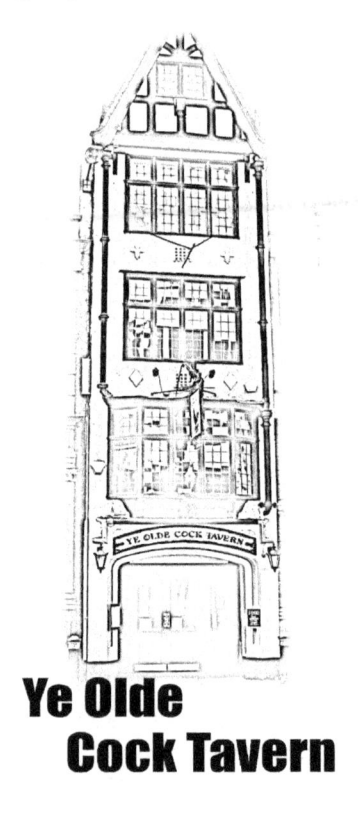

Ye Olde Cock Tavern

Paranormal - Tourist Guide To - London

Chapter 6
The Haunted Theatres

This has to be the section I was looking forward to writing and examining more than any other. London has the worlds greatest theatres, sorry to all my American readers yes Broadway is good, but London theatres are older, and have a much more varied history, and also put on more varied productions.

The reason I looked forward to this section more than any other is that I am a performer and used to specialise in musicals. Unfortunately due to knee injuries I had to cut back on my performing, but this did mean I became more and more involved in the world of the paranormal in between my acting work. The acting community is a very superstitious one and one theory is that the more creative people are more likely to see a ghost. This might mean that the more creative you are the more easily you hallucinate, or are conned by unscrupulous mediums and psychics. The other side of that coin is perhaps as a more creative type your mind is more open and that you may be in tune with other people and psychic events.

I will offer you theory its up to you what you decide, one thing you will notice with my books is that I always say that it is important to keep your mind open, not so open that your brain falls out, and also never assume you have an answer. Any medium, psychic, or sceptic that comes along and tells you they have the definitive answer to any ghost story, or life after death is wrong. Any scientist will tell you that an answer to a question is subject to the knowledge at our disposal. Medical practitioners years ago used to keep us healthy by balancing our humours and the established science community would have said that is exactly how it works. Years later we look back at this and say,

Paranormal - Tourist Guide To - London

"what were these idiots thinking?" It is only with the benefit of our knowledge that we can look at previous theories and say they are wrong.

I am sure in years to come that the brain will be understood so much better than it is today and we will have answers to the questions of what is a poltergeist, and what is an apparition. Until that time we have superstition, theory, and ghost spotters. The amateur ghost spotter is often caught unawares in a theatre, friends of mine have seen ghosts in theatres without looking for them. A colleague of mine was at a theatre and as she walked up the stairs she saw a figure standing there and thought he looked a bit weird, she looked away and looked back a second later and he was gone with no possible means of escape. The description she gave was the exact look attributed to a ghost seen in that building.

You also have the problem of ghost hunters seeing things and then possibly embellishing the story and possible mental health issues, do not forget the brain is easily confused. An eye witness is often the worst type of witness, so it is a good idea to have a camera with you at all times. One such ghost hunter that I know of claims to have seen a figure in a theatre and ignored it thinking it was a real person, he realised that there should not have been anyone there and looked back and the figure was gone. Now unfortunately this ghost hunter does get easily confused with reality, I think that is the politest way of saying it.

This man has given reports of events, and hauntings that he was witness to, and we know that he was not actually there. The problem is that we think that in his own head he believes the story happened to him, and it is his brain that is playing tricks on him, if he had taken a photo of the supposed spirit then his testament would have some weight, as it is the story is worse than useless, as not only does it not further the world of paranormal science but it also furthers his colleagues opinion that he might be mentally disturbed. Let's face it most of my friends think I am mad doing this for a living, I hope some day that I have enough evidence to push the general consciousness of the population and prove to them the paranormal is a real thing that surrounds them everyday. One community that does not need persuading is the theatrical community. You will rarely go into any theatre in the country that is more than 50 years old and not hear about a ghost. One such theatre is one of the oldest in the country and more importantly is possibly the most haunted one in the world the Theatre Royal in Drury Lane, but also we cannot forget one of the most famous theatrical ghouls that of the Phantom in Phantom of the Opera, as this production is also in a haunted theatre.

I could write an entire book on the haunted theatres in London so instead we shall mention a handful of the most famous ones, and then hopefully in the ensuing volumes of Paranormal London we can get through all of them.

Adelphi Theatre,

Location: 409 - 412 Strand
Nearest Underground Station: The nearest underground stations to the Adelphi Theatre are Covent Garden (Piccadilly line) and Charing Cross/Embankment (District, Circle, Northern and Bakerloo lines).
Website: www.reallyuseful.com/theatres/adelphi-theatre/

We have to mention the ghost of the actor William Terriss, as he is rather famous in the parapsychology world. Not because he was a particularly good or famous actor, and far be it from me to slander any ghosts acting skills, I am sure he was very good, but to parapsychologists he is more famous for haunting at least two different locations. A fellow actor stabbed him to death at the Stage Door in 1897, however it is not the stage door that the actor haunts, but instead it is the backstage areas, we will also hear about him as we go backstage at the Lyceum theatre as well, and we hear about him again in the London Underground.

ADELPHI THEATRE 1840

Obviously we performers are easily mentally disturbed as the murderer of William Terriss supposedly spent the remainder of his days in a mental institute after being deemed legally insane. Another strange actor that was in the theatre at the time of the William Terriss murder was his understudy. The day before the murder he claimed to have a dream where he saw Terriss lying in a pool of blood with blood oozing from a wound in William's chest.

Fortune Theatre

Location: Russell Street
Nearest Underground Station: Nearest underground station is Covent Garden (Piccadilly line).
Website: www.thewomaninblack.com/

I am going to mention this theatre partly because I saw an amazing show here, and it is one of the longest running plays in London theatrical history mostly because it is brilliant. The show is called 'The Woman In Black' and not only that, but the theatre has a ghost of a very similar nature.

Paranormal - Tourist Guide To - London

Featuring the amazing show – The Woman in Black, a 'must see' if you are in London

It is an amazing place to go and study the effect of mass psychology and also mass panic. If you sit in a cinema and watch a horror film you can see everyone jump or scream at the right points in unison. When the director wants you to scream he shows you what he wants you to see. In the theatre however the director does not have this privilege.

As theatre is live, the audience can look at what they want rather than where the camera has been positioned. It is a testament to the skill of the writing, directing, and acting talents in the production that means the audience is so engrossed with what is happening on stage that they look and concentrate on what is intended. As a parapsychologist however I love to watch the audience reaction to the parts that I know are likely to cause screams and scares. So if 'Woman in Black' is still on when you read this book I implore you to get a ticket.

But let us concentrate on the theatre's non intentional Black Lady. It is reported that a female figure clad in black is seen in the hospitality

Paranormal - Tourist Guide To - London

bar,and also in one of the boxes. If you are lucky the box will be empty during the performance as she reportedly sits watching the show.

One of the actors in the production reported seeing female figures at the side of the stage even though there was definitely no one actually there, another actress has reported feeling someone following her onto stage yet when she turned there was no one there.

Her Majesty's Theatre

Location: Haymarket
Nearest Underground Station: Nearest underground station is Piccadilly Circus (Piccadilly and Bakerloo lines).
Website: www.reallyuseful.com/theatres/her-majestys-theatre/

HER MAJESTY'S THEATRE

This has one of the most famous ghostly sights in the word. That of the Phantom in 'Phantom of the Opera' a musical that has taken more money in the box office worldwide than nearly every other musical that has ever been in the West End. Now before you quote me on that, that is obviously an overstatement, but regardless of whether you like it or not it has made a huge amount of money.

Enough of Lloyd Webber's show lets look at the theatre that it is housed in. Her Majesty's Theatre was built back in 1897 for the actor-manager Sir Beerbohm Tree and he actually made several appearances on his stage. He apparently liked to watch shows from his favourite place in the house which was the top box, stage right. We are told that this is the place which he likes to manifest in. He does not necessarily wait for the box to be empty either as occupants of the box complain of cold spots, and that the door to the box suddenly opens of its own accord, with no visible means.

If it is indeed Sir Beerbohm who is the ghost then he likes to keep his hand in and checks out the latest productions whenever he can. Back in the 1970's, during a performance of, 'Cause Celebre', the entire cast of the play watched the ghost walk across the theatre at the back of the stalls.

So which looks scarier me or the Phantom

Another great performer is said to haunt this stage, and that is the ghost of Tommy Cooper. The BBC broadcast a list of haunted theatres and stated that the spirit of Tommy had been seen by performers there, now if you are a foreign tourist and you are wondering who Tommy Cooper is, just ask anyone who is at least 30yrs old and they will tell you he was one of the funniest man who ever lived. He was a genius in the world of magic and I will not tell you anymore, just go on the internet and you will see hhis amazing skill and dexterity in the world of magic.

Lyceum Theatre

Location: Wellington Street
Nearest Underground Station: Covent garden
Website: www.lyceumtheatrelondon.com

A rather disturbing sight appears in this theatre, and more importantly this ghost chooses to sit in the cheaper seats. Now if I haunted a theatre I would at least make sure I got the best seats. Its not as if anyone is going to try and get you to move.

This sight however is rather disturbing so I cannot for one moment think that anyone would ask it to leave or even approach it, as It is an elderly women sitting stroking what appears to be a severed head.

No one can be sure about who the ghost is, or indeed who was the previous owner of the head, but it has been speculated that the woman may have been Madam Marie Tussaud with one of her famous waxwork heads. She showed her waxworks before she acquired a permanent venue at this theatre for their very first outing.

The origin of this story seems to date back about 150 years, in the late 1800's, a couple of theatre goers were sat in a box and were being stared at by the severed head on a ladies lap. There is a possible explanation for who the ghost actually was, and this was given by the ghost spotter. He was visiting a friend and he saw an old

Paranormal - Tourist Guide To - London

painting hanging on the wall, it happened to be that of a cavalier who was beheaded in the Civil War, and the family who owned the painting said that they think their ancestors owned the land that the theatre was now built on.

Another theory was that it was a wax head, for it was here that Madame Tussaud exhibited her first museum of wax celebrities. It is possible that the ghost of Madame Tussaud wanted to watch an opera whilst haunting, and just so happened to be in the middle of stock taking at the same time.

This is not the only spectre haunting the corridors and auditoriums of this great building, they have one of my favourite types of haunting that of a poltergeist. Poltergeist have always been my favourite, (and most terrifying) apparitions, most of the time when you see a ghost, you can possibly shrug it off and say that you are seeing things. It is a lot harder to dismiss a flying table zooming past your head. Poltergeists tend to start off small with rapping and knocking noises and then over a period of a few months build up to bigger and greater

Paranormal - Tourist Guide To - London

examples of phenomena, this one seems to have followed such a pattern.

This all started in the Royal Circle bar, as the knocking and tapping noises starting emanating from within the walls and furniture, these banging noises became louder and louder and then it became violent. Now I have never heard any credible stories of real harm being caused by ghosts, but occasionally you get stories of ghosts pushing and grabbing. Now this poltergeists seems to have been blamed for the pushing of staff in the stalls toilets. Now in my experience of hauntings they tend to stick to one small area, poltergeists can move about a bit more, but these may be two separate spooks, and there may be a third as well as the Grand Circle toilets has poltergeist activity, the most impressive of which involved all the toilet doors opening and closing, slamming and banging all at the same time. This was seen by staff and audience members together. Well lets hope it was during the interval or pre show, as I would not want to be the audience member going back to my seat amid murmurs of discontent from the audience thinking it was me making all that noise.

The spooks in this theatre have a tendency to haunt toilets, as one cleaner was checking the Royal Circle toilets one morning when one of the doors swung wide open and the spectre of a woman walked in, he reported that it was dressed in a long grey coat and bonnet, she walked into the cubicle and disappeared. As most people do he seemed to try and rationalise this sighting and it looks like he thought it may have been a real person as he reported it to security, who told him that the building was empty.

This may have been the ghost of Lady Irving, for this was the theatre that the late great actor Sir Henry Irving worked in, and the legendary writer Bram Stoker, of Dracula fame, also worked here. In fact it is rumoured that he based his Dracula character on Sir Henry Irving himself. He was supposedly an alcoholic with Brandy being his favourite tipple, in real lief he supposedly found a novel way of stopping himself drinking, and that was to knock over the brandy glass. Well this glass destroying hobby of his seems to have carried over into the afterlife, and the staff there claim that whenever a Brandy glass is placed on the side bar it will fly off, and they say that is why there are no Brandy glasses in the theatre today.

Staff have reported experiencing an oppressive feeling or the sense theatre being followed or watched whilst walking up and down the corridors of the building and perhaps they are being pursued by a ghost that is no longer visible. There was once a spook that resembled a corpse like man roaming the corridors of the building. This ghoul seems to have left back in 1945 when the building became a dance hall, and has not been reported since. If my research is wrong however and he has been spotted feel free to email me so I can update my records. Many ghost stories change and develop over time, and the best thing we can do as researchers is keep up to date with the tales so always feel free to contact me or your local ghost hunting group with sightings, we never treat you like you are mad, (even if you are) and every reputable paranormal group treats your report with respect and annonymity. So should you be sat in the theatre watching some fantastic musical and the people around you are zombies, with a weak bladder, and people with a head on their lap then do try and get some contact details from them.

The Theatre Royal

Location: Drury Lane
Nearest Underground Station: Nearest underground station is Covent Garden (Piccadilly line).
Website: www.reallyuseful.com/theatres/theatre-royal-drury-lane

This theatre has a history of putting on some of the worlds longest running musicals and in recent years was the home to Miss Saigon the Producers, and Lord of The Rings. One of the ghosts here must have had a bit of a hand in the success of some of these shows, and also many others around the country. One famous story that seems to have possibly originated here is the story of a ghost that watches dress rehearsals and opening nights, if the ghost is seen in the auditorium you can guarantee hat you have a success on your hands. So Miss Saigon may have to thank this ghost for it's success rather

Paranormal - Tourist Guide To - London

than the songs of Boublil and Schoenberg.

We shall come to this ghost later as we talk more about the spirits but I include him here, as a similar story is told in many other theatres around the city, and even the world, so he may be modern folklore, superstition, or even wishful thinking causing hallucinations in a rather exhausted and nervous cast.

DRURY LANE 1850

There has been a theatre on this site since the year 1661 and most of this building dates from 1812 which makes it one of the oldest as well as most haunted theatres in the world.

Most of the ghosts in theatres tend to be of a benevolent nature, and often very helpful. Perhaps if you believe in spirits returning then these are likely to be performers, actors, singers, or even theatre goers that are returning to help out.

The Man in Grey

This theatre has had the odd entry in the Guinness book of records, with longest running shows, largest audiences, most performances etc. However that is a title that swaps around the theatres depending on the success of a show with Les Miserables currently in lead on most of those records. By the time you read this book if it stays in print long enough then the worlds longest running musical might be "Ross Andrews the Parapsychologist – the Musical!" fair enough it's highly unlikely but in the world of the paranormal stranger things have happened.

Paranormal - Tourist Guide To - London

*If you want to see something really scary
then SHREK the musical should do it,
how that show managed to be a hit on Broadway is truly paranormal.*

The man in grey mat have originated in this theatre wishing his good luck upon a show, and cast as e mentioned earlier, but he definitely is responsible for what might be the Guinness book of records highest number of people seeing a ghost simultaneously in a building. Back in 1939 there were reportedly over 70 people on stage for a photo session before the show "The Dancing Years" opened and all of them saw this grey figure walk through the auditorium, in the upper circle. Many reports of this ghost all say the same thing that this man in grey dressed in 18th century clothing walks along the back of the upper circle then disappears. Some reports are not so distinct, other times it has been reported that the figure appears a mist, one famous ghost report claimed to have seen a blue mist taking the same path as the man in grey.

Many famous ghost hunters throughout history have taken these tales very seriously and there have been a large amount of investigations into this building from some of the great historical parapsychologist like Harry Price, they may have been deluded, but there have been so many sightings for them to take it seriously.

One cleaner reported seeing a man sat in one of the seats on her first

Paranormal - Tourist Guide To - London

day working at the theatre, she was rather confused and gave a description of the gentleman and the rest of the staff told her not to worry as she had just described the ghost perfectly. One possible explanation for who he is, is the actor Arnold Woodruffe but we shall come onto him later.

If you do get to see a show in this theatre try and get a seat in the upper circle in Row D preferably the second seat from the end, as it is reportedly this seat where he has been seen.

Dan Leno

Theatres like to have their share of famous ghosts, and there is no point in have a ghost of on famous actor, its much better to have a famous one helping out. One such ghost is a very famous actor, and comedian by the name of Dan Leno, who haunts the backstage area, and his footsteps are heard. Footsteps are weird enough though this is possibly a noise from another part of the building transferring along corridors and echoing halls, but the other noise is more distinct and linked specifically to Dan Leno, the sound of clog dancing has been heard coming from empty dressing rooms. Many actors have claimed to feel his presence on stage and also that they have smelt the distinctive scent of lavender which apparently Dan Leno famously always wore.

Joe Grimaldi

Another famous name that haunts the theatre is the world famous clown Joseph Grimaldi, he is so famous that the clown makeup design that we know of today was invented by Grimaldi. He seems to help out with some positive encouragement to actors and performers that are not giving their best, by supposedly kicking them in the bottom. This ghost has been experienced many times, and possibly more times than is reported. I am sure that if an actor knows the story and then they are unlikely to tell anyone, as that means admitting that you are either not very good, or you were being lazy and not trying your best.

Paranormal - Tourist Guide To - London

A Helping Hand

One of these spirits may also be the helping hand that has been mentioned and reported by confused actors. Now for those of us who work in the theatre a confused actor is nothing uncommon. The reason for the confusion is much more interesting to parapsychologists. Sometimes actors are stood backstage and happen to be in the way or in the wrong place, sometimes an actor is stood in the wings (side of the stage) and without realising it they can be seen by members of the audience who are sat near the edges of the auditorium it is then that a helping hand pushes or moves the actors to the place they should be stood. The offending actor then turns to thank or find out who helped, and there is no one there.

He also reportedly helps out by moving actors to better angles and positions whilst they are on stage performing, so if you see an actor suddenly look shocked and start looking around themselves they may have been grabbed by the ghost.

Charles Macklin

One ghost supposed to roam around the theatre, he was an Irish actor who died in July 1797 after a fight with Arnold Woodruffe. Arnold is supposed to haunt the building as well, seeking forgiveness but the theory is that Charles keeps him trapped in the theatre, as their ongoing feud continues.

Mediums have claimed that Arnold was jealous of Charles, and that Charles was a bit of Diva and rather egotistical, a fight broke put between them, and the story is that Charles was stabbed, some people say that Arnold stabbed him in the side, and another tale is that Arnold stabbed him in the eye with a cane and this is what killed him.

Arnold, it has been said, is the ghost that is the helping hand, and other people claim that it is Grimaldi that is the helping hand, I guess we hall never know unless we manage to see both of them at the same time.

The Man in Chains

There is no surprise that a theatrical ghost likes to be theatrical, and this one most definitely does. He walks around carrying chains and the sound has also been captured on recordings. The only way this could be any more theatrical would be if the ghost was wearing a white sheet making, 'Wooo!' noises as well.

This ghost has been seen in the front of house areas and on the staircases, so if you want to do a spot of impromptu ghost hunting then come in to the foyer and pretend to buy a ticket whilst looking towards the staircases and making audio recordings. What I will suggest is actually buying a ticket as I have never seen a bad show at this theatre, and a show in the Theatre Royal Drury Lane is almost like a mark of quality virtually guaranteed to give you a good night out.

One witness to this spirit was the television show, 'Most Haunted'. For those readers that do not know this show, a group of ghost hunters go into a haunted building and film for 24 hours to see if they can find anything. I do know people that have worked for this show and as they say you have to remember that it is for entertainment and for television so they do tend to make things look exciting even if they were not. This lead to ask the question, "You mean they fake things?". I was reassured that they do not, and that they have genuinely been very scared in some locations, and that the screams are real.

The ghost is apparently somewhere between 5'7" and 5'9" he wears a cap, is slightly overweight dressed in dark clothing and is carrying a load of chains. To me this sounds like a theatre technician, the chains being the safety chains that are attached to lights. These safety chains are immensely important as I can personally verify. I was up a small scaffolding tower that was on wheels putting some lights onto a lighting grid about forty foot above a stage. Thankfully I had just put one of these chains around a lighting bar and still had hold of it, the wheel on the bottom of the scaffolding tower gave way (I obviously had too many cakes for dinner) and the tower fell over. Thankfully I still had my hand threaded throw this chain and I was hanging from the lighting rig for about ten seconds whilst a colleague was frantically moving a large 'A' framed ladder across the stage to me.

Technicians are a strange type that skulk around in the dark so it may well be that most of these sightings are technicians trying not to be seen whilst they go about their daily work, but a lot of the sightings are by staff who would recognise other members of staff.

This can be discounted when you do not see the entire person and I was sent some amazing footage from the same TV show where all the group saw was a pair of legs walking along a staircase.

We must always always remember that a theatre is a place of illusion, a place where your perception of reality is purposefully played with and distorted, so we must always treat these places with scepticism. When a ghost story is reported over and over again however we have to start looking at the tales and say to ourselves, "What is it that is causing these people to experience the same phenomena.?"

*Try and find this landmark at the Theatre,
it's a bit easier to spot than a ghost*

Paranormal - Tourist Guide To - London

Chapter 7
The Underground

So why is the underground haunted? Do we just have a fear of being underground, the fact that we cannot see the outside, and that we are trapped in the tunnels. Maybe it is because during the construction of these tunnels many people died, or that there have been suicides, or that graveyards, and plague pits were moved to make way for the tunnels. Some of the underground stations, and tunnels are actually cutting straight through large plague pits. It is highly likely that half dead, yet still actually living breathing victims of the black death were thrown into these pits and buried alive.

If you believe that the ghosts are spirits of the dead coming back to haunt places that they suffered or died in then you do not need to go far into the underground to find disturbing unexplained tales.

If you have ever had to catch the tube late at night on the last trains you know that it can be a very scary place, but you do not need to worry as there are CCTV cameras all over the entire system. These cameras have several times thrown up some very strange phenomena.

BAKERLOO LINE - *I bet he didn't pay for a ticket*

If you are planning on ghost hunting around London don't forget to travel on the Bakerloo line and head Northbound. There is a story about a traveller that may join you.

You won't see him, not directly, but you may see him sat next to you as you catch his reflection in the window.

BANK - *knock, knock, who's there?*

About one hundred years ago, many of the former residents were evicted from this station. These former tenants did not really object too much as they were dead, and had been for some time. One of the entrances to the station used to be an entrance to a church crypt, and in 1900 the dead were moved along the line to somewhere else. Perhaps the ghosts in this station are just trying to find their coffins once more, and have a decent nights sleep.

One worker in this station tells a story about how he was working the night shift and he was locking up one night, he looked around all the lifts to shut them down, and as he walked away from lift one, which he had just checked, he heard several clear distinct knocking noises. This he found very strange, he had just checked to see if there was anyone in there, and more importantly that lift had not been used that day.

He was not particularly happy about this and moved away rather quickly, not daring to look back. He went to the switch room and wedged the door open. He turned off the lights leaving just the emergency work lights on for him to leave by, and walked away. It seems our spirit was not happy at being ignored as the door that he had wedged open slammed shut behind him. The worker did not stick around to find out what had slammed the door as he ran rather fast out of the station.

Yes of course this could be perfectly normal, we could just say there was an unexplained random noise and a draught caused a door to slam. What we need to realise is that this worker had been there for a while, and he knew the ins and outs of the station. These people know the noises, they know the draughts, creaks, and strange knocks, and when they tell you it is a noise that should not be there I personally believe them.

Paranormal - Tourist Guide To - London

BANK MONUMENT STATION - *Sarah is sightseeing*

One worker had closed the station and was checking his CCTV cameras, at about 2 am he noticed a figure on one of the screens. She looked like a little old lady standing in a long corridor. He grabbed his radio and headed off, constantly staying in contact with another colleague. As he got near where she was she looked and and straight at him. She then headed off around a corner,and he ran after her. As he walked around the corner she was nowhere to be seen. He quickly called his colleague to check the cameras and there was no little old lady to be found. We scoured every possible place she could have been, all the corridors and ways in and out were locked and barred. There was no possible way this woman could have got out of the station.

Now why have we called this woman Sarah? One possible explanation of who this figure may be is a woman called Sarah Whitehead. She was a rather sad woman who every day walked the Bank area, dressed all in black, mourning for her executed brother who was killed in 1811. It is believed that she was buried in the area,and that her grave was disturbed during the construction of the Bank station.

BECONTREE STATION - *are you looking at me?*

One worker here was working late into the evening and was about to go home, as he was working he heard a door nearby rattle. This did not disturb him to much as this door often rattled when a train was coming. He became slightly disturbed when he heard it a second time, yet there was still no train. By the time he heard the third rattle he had become rather unnerved.

He walked away confused and thinking hard about what could have caused this, it was not long before he found out. He walked upstairs to chat to another member of staff and as he walked along the platform he felt as though there was someone else on the platform with him. He turned around and there stood behind him was a woman, yet it looked like she had no face. It was not long before he reached the other member of staff. The work colleague turned to him and said,

"You look as if you have seen a ghost"

the obvious answer came flying back that he had indeed seen a ghost. Instead of then giving a description of what he had seen The work colleague asked if it looked like a woman in white with no face. The initial man was obviously even more confused, and enquired as to how did he know this. It transpired that this colleague had also seen the phantom figure.

BETHNAL GREEN - *the screams*

The staff had all left apart from one member of staff, and he sat there doing some paperwork, yet he was disturbed by the sound of what he described as children crying. He dismissed this thinking that it was nothing and some weird anomalous noise. The noise became impossible to ignore as the crying soon became swamped by the noise of distressed women and panicking people screaming. This seemed to go on for about 15 minutes. He left his office and walked out to the booking hall because he was so scared.

This may well be an excellent example of a 'stone tape' type haunting. Where the atmosphere has somehow captured an event and is replaying it over and over again. This may well be the reconstruction of the events in the second world war where 173 people were crushed to death in the station. The worst civilian disaster in the whole of the war. We have been told that out of the 173 people that were killed 143 of them were women and children which lends some form of validity to this claim, as it was mostly women and children that the witness claims to have heard.
I am often asked why do these ghosts only haunt at night time? Why does it not happen in the day? In reference to these ghosts it is easy to see why no one picks up on these events in the daytime. Any audio phenomena in the daytime when the tube is being used would be instantly ignored. The theory that a ghost has to be recognised before

Paranormal - Tourist Guide To - London

it can become strong comes into play here, if the first subtle noises are ignored as a child crying or moaning somewhere then perhaps the stone tape stops there. If the noises are acknowledged then perhaps the tap keeps playing. On a busy day in the underground people are far too preoccupied with themselves and their problems to wonder about any strange noses.

COVENT GARDEN - *famous yet rare*

One of the most famous ghost stories is that of the Covent Garden ghost, yet it has been a while since it has been seen, or at least reported to have been seen. One guard was locking up late at night, and he turned around to see a tall man in a waistcoat. He apologised to the tall man thinking that he had somehow locked him in the station. He turned around to open the doors and then realised the man had gone.

Another colleague later showed him a photo of an actor called William Terriss, the only problem was that this man had been stabbed to death years before. As far back as 1897 to be precise.

It must be very frustrating that an actor is more famous as a ghost, and remembered for his hauntings rather than for his art back when he was alive.

FARINGDON STATION - *yet more screams*

We have a ghost with a name here – Anne Naylor. Apparently Anne was only 13 when she was murdered by a mother and daughter team, they worked in the Milliners tht stood where the station now stands.

Even though she was a murder victim in the18th Century, (supposedly in the area that is the platform of the station) it is her screams that are still reported to echo around when there is no alive person here.

Paranormal - Tourist Guide To - London

HYDE PARK CORNER - *the ever escalating escalator*

In an energy conscious world we obviously do not wish to use electricity when it is not needed. One worker tells a story about ghost power could be the answer to all our energy needs. One night he was going round locking up and closing the station down, in doing this he not only locked doors, but shut down the escalator. To do this he had to remove the 'breakers' this means that the escalator cannot move.

At about half past two he heard a commotion, and with a colleague he walked out to the ticket area, and he noticed the escalator had started and was moving. This is technically impossible without replacing the breakers which he had definitely not done. They shut everything down again and returned to the staffroom. As he was making a coffee he felt as if someone was standing and looking at him, he turned around to see his colleague looking rather shaken. When he asked what was wrong thinking that his friend was feeling ill, his work colleague asked him if he had seen the face.

Apparently a face had come out of the wall and stared at him. Soon after this they left work, and his friend never returned to work in the underground again.

KENNINGTON LOOP - *the invisible passenger*

My plan in this book was to tell you all about the ghosts that you can have a chance of seeing, this one however you probably will never get a chance to see. I will include this story as I am told that the Kennington Loop is notoriously haunted. The question I can now hear you all screaming is, 'What is the Kennington Loop?'

This is a section of the track near Kennington Station where there have been more reports of unusual phenomena than anywhere else. The loop is there as it means that trains can turn around and head back north again. The Kennington station is where the line ends for a lot of the routes so that all the passengers can get off and the train can then enter the loop to turn around. This does mean that often the train will wait up to fifteen minutes before it is in use again.

One day the line controller asked a driver to divert to Kennington loop, this he did and sat there waiting for quite a while, about 5 or 10 minutes. I know that does seem long but when you sat quietly in a dark tunnel that can seem a long time. When you are sat quietly with nothing to do, your senses become very attuned to their surroundings, the driver heard the clicking of the inter connecting doors opening and closing in his train as though someone was walking between carriages.

This should not have been possible as all the passengers had gotten off of the train at Kennington. The train had been checked that there was no one left on it, so this was very bizarre. The train was then examined again and no one could be found yet many of the interconnecting doors had been opened as though someone had walked along the carriages.

The story is that a man had tried to board the train at Kennington in between the cars and had got dragged onto the track and into the sidings where he died. This experience was not a one off, and has happened on more than one occasion.

LIVERPOOL STREET STATION - *the man in white*

Way back in 2003 one of the controllers watching the CCTV coverage noticed a man standing on the platform he found this rather strange as it was two in the morning, and there should not have been anyone there. The controller contacted a fellow worker that was near the area and told him that he had seen a man wearing white overalls standing near the east bound tunnel. The other working walked down to the aforementioned area and saw nothing he did a thorough investigation all around, and failed to find anyone.

The co worker then radioed back to the camera office and said that he failed to see anyone. This however came as rather a shock as the

Paranormal - Tourist Guide To - London

man sat in front of the cameras said that he could see the co worker walking around and that the figure in white was stood right next to him at one point. He walked back to the platform and looked around again,and yet again saw nothing. The camera operator however insists that whilst this co worker was walking around, the man in white was only yards away from him.

As the co worker turned and walked away, he turned and saw a set of white overalls on the bench behind him. This seemed to shock him more as he had not seen the overalls before that, and definitely he would have heard and seen someone if they had tried to sneak up on him.

Another interesting snippet of information to go with this sighting was some news I was given about some recent excavations above the tunnels. During the building work several hundred un-coffined bodies were found and it was said that they were so tightly packed that there were as many as eight bodies per cubic metre unceremoniously crammed together.

I included this story because it shows a rather unusual phenomena. Most of the time when cameras are involved, it is the camera that does not see the spectre, and the human does. This has lead us to many very reasonable assumptions and theories that the ghost is not necessarily seen with the eye.

The theory is that the brain is affected by other stimuli and recreates the image irrespective of what the eye sees. This well respected theory unfortunately gets thrown out of the window with stories like these ones, where the camera sees the image and the human does not. As always happens with ghosts the video footage does not exist, as the video system was not actually recording apparently, or if it was then the tape no longer exists.

Paranormal - Tourist Guide To - **London**

Chapter 8
The Haunted Church

Yet again I will do my disclaimer here, yes I know of many haunted churches in the Capital but I will only put a few in here, so that we have a taste of every type of haunted venue that we can find. Here are some of the really famous stories, and easier accessible churches.

ST. BARTHOLOMEW THE GREAT,

Location: West Smithfield, London, EC1A 7DQ
Opening times:
Monday - Friday 8.30 am to 5.00 pm (4pm from 11th November to 14th February)
Saturday 10.30 am to 4.00 pm Sunday 8.30 am to 8.00 pm
Tourist visits and guided parties are not permitted during services. The Church is closed for a few days after Christmas, except for Sunday morning services.
Price: They have an unusual charging policy, most churches have free entry and encourage a set donation so here is what was written on their website

Admission Charges

There is a charge for tourist visits to St Bartholomew's. There is no charge for admission for the first hour or for those coming solely for prayer and private devotion, for which the Chapel of the Holy Icon of the Mother of God is set aside.
| Adults | £4.00 |
| Concessions | £3.50 |

Paranormal - Tourist Guide To - London

Pre-booked Groups	£3.50
Educational Groups	Leader free & students at £3.00 each if pre-booked a institution provided to confirm it is a course-related v
Family Ticket	£10.00 (2 adults & 1-3 children)
Adult Season Ticket	£30 (for one year)
Photography	£1

Nearest Underground Station: Barbican, St Paul's, Farringdon.
Website: www.greatstbarts.com

Not just a haunted church but one of the oldest ones in the city, as it was founded way back in 1123 by Rahere. I find this person rather intriguing he was a pious holy man when he wore one hat, but he had another hat and that had bells on it, for he was the jester to King Henry I. I am sure that he did not do both jobs at the same time, however laughable some people find religion now back in the twelfth century it was a slightly more serious matter. He apparently received a vision of St.Bartholomew whilst on a pilgrimage to Rome. This vision apparently instructed him to build both a church and a hospital at Smithfield.

Rahere changed his jesting hat for a monks outfit, and after spending the rest of his life in the service of the church he was buried inside the church in an rather ornate tomb. Perhaps he is objecting to the design of his tomb, or perhaps it is because he loved the church so much that he returns. He is often seen near the altar, or walking towards or near the Lady chapel. One of the reasons given for the appearance of the ghost of Rahere is that his tomb was disturbed during the 19th Century. The church authorities decided they wanted to see how much the body had deteriorated. This may seem weird and rather gory to us, but his is not that unusual throughout history, and many churches have used well preserved corpses as a grisly tourist trap for people to venerate saints.

Apparently the body was well preserved, and the clothing was still virtually intact including the sandals. One of the church warders fell ill and he then confessed that he had stolen one of the sandals from the

Paranormal - Tourist Guide To - London

corpse of Rahere, after returning it he then got better. Personally I think that it was no so much a cursed sandal causing problems, more like bacteria from the rotting feet of a rather grotesque foot. The sandal however was not actually returned to the corpse's foot, and stories are abound that Rahere is looking for his lost shoe. Rahere is seen as a cowled figure walking around the building, and gliding through the shadows. When people have seen him they say that often it is accompanied by a sense of well being, and he often disappears next to the lady chapel.

Another ghost is supposed to be that of a priest that was burned alive in a cage during the reign of Henry VIII but I have not managed to find anyone who can verify any sightings,or audio of this figure.

When it comes to audio however there are some excellent reports of phantom organ music suddenly striking up, event though there is no one touching the organ. Should you get any organs on tape whilst here I would love to hear them..... That sounds a lot worse than it was meant to, I mean musical organs obviously! Now go and remove your minds from the gutter and start looking for more ghosts.

So if you have your camera and have a night vision capability point it in all these directions whilst pretending to be deep in contemplation. The problem with churches is very often they object to ghost hunting, and if they don't their congregation often do. I have often been accused of dabbling in things I do not comprehend, and that I am doing the work of the devil. I agree I do not fully comprehend the world of the paranormal, so therefore I do this to try and bring some scientific rigour to the world of superstition. If we had taken this attitude with anything that we do not understand then we would have no penicillin, no mobile phones, no cars, no ... well the list is pretty endless, but let us also add 'no intelligence'.

Without progression we either stand still or we regress. As to the charge of doing the devil's work, well Lucifer is the bringer of light, hence matches being called Lucifers. The light which he brought refers to the acquisition of knowledge and enlightenment so I guess at a basic level, yes I must be.

Paranormal - Tourist Guide To - London

About the Author

Ross Andrews has written many books, and articles for magazines, radio and TV about the paranormal, and has many years experience In the field of parapsychology or 'spook spotting' as he calls it.

I have no idea why when I get to this bit of my books I write in the third person so instead I will carry on as me. Hello again so what do I write this time, it does seem very egotistical to write in every book a new chapter about myself, but I know there are a lot of people out there who read my books. Since the last book I have encountered many a spook, some excellent new recordings and footage from the worlds most haunted building (St.Briavel's castle in the Forest of Dean). I have had some interesting experiences in some of the scary locations in the worlds most haunted village (Prestbury, not Pluckley as is often claimed, Prestbury has more ghosts per square mile than any other village). There have been a few more radio shows, and the occasional TV contribution, and more and more stories keep flooding in to me.

For those of you who have read my previous books you will know I am always after more stories so feel free to email them to me .
ghostnight@hotmail.co.uk

A brief history of me for new readers - Born in 1972, always had weird paranormal things happen near or around me, and for the last twenty years I have investigated the paranormal wherever possible. I was chairman of the paranormal science group Parasoc - The Myers Society. With a few ghost hunting colleagues in 2005 I set up a group called Phantomfest so we could take members of the public into various haunted buildings, which we still do from time to time – phantomfest@hotmail.co.uk - if you want to know more, just email me.

Paranormal - Tourist Guide To - London

I am well aware that this book maybe in print still in fifty years time and I apologise now if the internet information is no longer relevant.

If after, or during your explorations of London because of this book you experience anything paranormal please email me s I would love to update our readers on the stories. It is always better to give recent stories wherever possible, there are so many tales that I get given that are from a ghost sighting that happened fifty or sixty years ago, contemporary stories are always more interesting.

So ego boost over let us, without further ado, get out there and do some ghost hunting.

Paranormal - Tourist Guide To - London

Further reading, and thanks

Further Excellent Books to Read on the Subject

In the process of writing this book, many newspaper articles were read, internet sites trawled, and witnesses spoken to. There are countless stories I had to miss out just because of space restrictions in this book, This is by no means a definitive study of ghosts in the area, more stories flood in every week and hopefully these will see the light of day in a future book. If you have any interesting stories or hauntings to tell me about please feel free to contact me on my emai address ghostnight@hotmail.co.uk . Until that time then I recommend reading through some of these titles.

Andrews, Ross, - Paranormal Cheltenham, Paranormal Forest of Dean, Paranormal Oxford, St.Briavel's Castle The Most Haunted Building in the World
Cameron, Janet, - Paranormal Brighton and Hove
Ritson, Darren, - In Search of Ghosts: Real Hauntings From Around Britain
Playfair, Guy Lyon – The House is Haunted
Ian John Shillito, & Becky Walsh – Haunted West End Theatres
Walking Haunted London – Richard Jones
Ghosts of London – Jack Hallam
Ghosts of London – J.A.Brooks

Another interesting site to visit especially if its near Halloween is - www.londonparanormal.com - as they run the London Paranormal festival.

Email ghostnight@hotmail.co.uk to be able to report any of your findings whilst researching London ghosts for yourself. If you want to go ghost hunting and are too scared to just head out and try it alone, then look at the ghostnight.org website join a ghost hunt and who knows you may end up featuring in my next book.

See you all in the next book with many more true stories to scare you to sleep

Paranormal - Tourist Guide To - **London**

YES I KNOW!

We did not write about St.Paul's, or the Tower of London, or Jack the Ripper, or The Enfield Poltergeist.

There is a reason for this, we have endeavoured to try and keep these guidebooks cheap and affordable to all ghost hunters and tourists, so this is the first in a range of books. If we put all the stories, and grainy ghost photo's into one book then it would be very heavy and thousands of pages long.

The point of this is to be able to use it and carry it round with you when you visit these premises.

More importantly however is that I need your feedback we need to hear your ghost stories, and include them in future books, especially if you have visited the premises in this publication and have more to add, we want to keep updating the tales with all the most recent hauntings. (ghostnight@hotmail.co.uk)

So have fun ghost hunting, remember the prices and opening hours are just a guide, and you should check before visiting, and most importantly remember...

GHOST ARE DEFINATELY REAL!

First published 2011
TozMusic Cheltenham
copyright Ross Andrews 2011
The right of Ross Andrews to be identified as author of this work has been asserted in accordance with the Copyrights, Designs, and Patents Act 1988

CPSIA information can be obtained
at www.ICGtesting.com
Printed in the USA
LVHW081319261118
598282LV00011B/192/P

9 781481 893701